Thrive on the changes
in your life !

Nate

Booth

THRIVING ON

The Art of Using Change to Your Advantage

CHANGE

"This practical and inspirational tool will provide you with the insights and techniques to confront and embrace change with greater ease and effectiveness. It is a valuable resource for anyone who wants to succeed and thrive in the future."

JACK CANFIELD
Co-author, *Chicken Soup for the Soul*

"I can safely predict that over the next ten years you and your customers will experience more change than you have ever experienced in your lifetime. The ability to master change has become a vital business and personal necessity. *Thriving on Change* is a stimulating and practical approach to the art of utilizing change to your advantage!"

DANIEL BURRUS
Leading technology forecaster & author, *Technotrends*

"Anyone who wants to master change will benefit from reading *Thriving on Change*."

ROBERT KRIEGEL, PH.D.
Author, *Sacred Cows Make the Best Burgers*

"*Thriving on Change* will help you create a magnificent future and lifestyle—for yourself, those you love, and our world. It's full of brilliant, thought-provoking insights."

MARK VICTOR HANSEN
Co-author, *Chicken Soup for the Soul*

"Change is not a choice; it is mandatory. Dr. Booth's enlightening book, *Thriving on Change*, will give you ideas and inspiration so that you can use change to your advantage."

FRAN TARKENTON
NFL Hall of Fame quarterback, speaker, entrepreneur

"Change—there's never been more. So there's never been a better reason to read Dr. Nate Booth's book, *Thriving on Change!*"

W. MITCHELL
Author, *The Man Who Would Not Be Defeated*

"Dr. Booth's book shows us how to make change our ally rather than our enemy. It's a 'must read' for everyone!"

DR. TONY ALESSANDRA
Author, *The Platinum Rule*, *People Smarts*, and *Communicating at Work*

"When you read this book, you will immediately be able to thrive on the constant change around you. Dr. Booth has packed *Thriving on Change* with dozens of practical methods you can use tomorrow to improve your life!"

KEN DYCHTWALD, PH.D.
Author, *Age Wave*

"*Change* is generally considered to be one of the most frightening words in our vocabulary. Nate's book helps us to realize that change is a natural part of our development and that it can be a great tool for growth, a means for expansion, and the key to personal and business success."

ANTHONY ROBBINS
Author, *Awaken the Giant Within* and *Unlimited Power*

HARRISON ACORN PRESS
9191 Towne Centre Drive, Suite 600
San Diego, CA 92122

Copyright © 1997 by Nate Booth

Although the author and publisher have made every effort to ensure the accuracy
and completeness of the information contained in this book,
we assume no responsibility for errors, inaccuracies, omissions, or any inconsistency herein.
Any slights of people, places, or organizations are unintentional.

Designed by Robert Mott and Kathy Wise for Robert Mott & Associates
Illustrated by Jesse Karras
Edited by Just Write

First printing 1997
1   2   3   4   5   6   7   8   9   10
ISBN 0-96499500-0-6
Library of Congress Card No. 95-82066

ATTENTION CORPORATIONS, UNIVERSITIES,
COLLEGES, AND PROFESSIONAL ORGANIZATIONS:
Quantity discounts are available on bulk purchases of this book for educational or
training purposes. Special books or book excerpts can also be created to fit specific needs.
For information, please contact Harrison Acorn Press, 9191 Towne Centre Drive,
Suite 600, San Diego, CA 92122, or call 619-535-6290.

THRIVING ON

The Art of Using Change to Your Advantage

CHANGE

Dr. Nate Booth

HARRISON ACORN PRESS
San Diego, California

Dedication

To my first and best teachers,

my parents, Bob and Mary Lou Booth,

who taught me how to

constantly learn and grow.

To my sister and brothers,

Linda, Sandy, and Randy,

who taught me how to

live together in (relative) harmony.

Finally, to the most important people in my life,

my wife Dawn

and my children

Chris, Emily, and Belinda,

who are teaching me how to

live, laugh, and love each day.

CONTENTS

Acknowledgments

I guess it runs in the family. For most of his life my grandfather, Jack Harrison, was the publisher of a small newspaper, the Oakland, Iowa *Acorn*. My Uncle John worked side by side with him and then went on to teach journalism, first at Penn State and later at Iowa University. My Dad published rural directories for over fifty years. And one day, I just "happened" to get the urge to write a book!

This book is the distillation of years of living, learning, starting over, shifting gears, and realigning my own path. It seemed I needed a lot of "real world" experience in making practical sense of the subject of change! The result—both what you see on the following pages, and what my life has become in the process—has been a journey filled with great demands and significant rewards, and I am grateful for all the assistance I have had along the way.

The people I would like to acknowledge are a diversified and caring bunch. My parents Bob and Mary Lou Booth created a "Beaver Cleaver" home in Harlan, Iowa for myself, my sister Linda, and my brothers Sandy and Randy. To this day, the time spent with them is one of the highlights of my life.

In addition to the aforementioned Uncle John, I would like to acknowledge my other aunts and uncles—John's wife Shirley, George and Helen Booth, and Nat and Elizabeth Booth. They all provided me with excellent role models of thriving on change.

My wife Dawn and my children Chris, Emily, and Belinda have put up with my unusually convoluted passage through life. I will always be thankful for their love, understanding, and support.

In 1987, I began working with a man who taught me the unlimited power of passion blended with compassion. Anthony Robbins and his wife Becky are my role models for living and giving on a global scale, and I'm grateful for their presence in my life.

Each year, I present over one hundred training programs in corporations and associations around the world. I would like to acknowledge everyone who attended those programs and contributed their time, energy, focus, and sometimes their stories. We were all teachers and students of each other.

I would also like to recognize the people who arrange my programs, especially the teams at Five Star Speakers and Trainers, Leading Authorities, The Harry Walker Agency, American Speakers Bureau, Walters Speakers Bureau, Speak Inc., The Speakers Bureau, Nationwide Speakers Bureau, Nightingale-Conant Speakers Bureau, Tarkenton Speakers Bureau, Rocky Mountain Speakers Bureau, Prism Speakers Bureau, International Speakers Bureau, Solomon Speakers Bureau, North American Speakers Bureau, and Lordly and Dame. Without their assistance, I would not have had the opportunity to meet so many people who are successfully managing change.

I would like to thank the past and present teams at Robbins Research International, Inc. for their support, most notably my partner, Penny Morris. She and they are the epitome of dedication.

The co-creators of this book deserve special recognition. David Christel helped me turn concepts and ideas into written words and visual concepts. As editors, Vicki St. George and her colleagues at Just Write polished, revised, and reviewed to make sure I said what I meant and meant what I said! Robert Mott was his usual creative genius with layout guidance and cover design, and Jesse Karras's cartoons contribute vividly to the feeling of this book. The wonderful people at About Books, Inc., and my friends Larry Michel and Frank Candy gave me the timely advice I needed to stay relatively sane.

Finally, I would like to acknowledge *you*! The average American reads less than one nonfiction book a year, and 58% of all Americans never read a nonfiction book after high school. By reading *Thriving on Change*, you have demonstrated your willingness to invest your time and money in order to learn and grow. You deserve all the abundance our rapidly changing world has to offer!

Foreword

In my long association with Dr. Booth, I've had the pleasure of working closely with him to create a series of corporate programs focusing on the one "constant" in our fast-paced world: change. The ability to harness the awesome power of change makes the crucial difference between people and companies who merely survive and those who achieve great success, today and in the decades to come.

Peak performers in all walks of life—CEOs like Bill Gates, national leaders like Nelson Mandela, humanitarian models like Mother Teresa, and the unnumbered individuals who produce outstanding results, quietly and effectively, in every corner of the world—share one essential trait. *They use the power of change to shape the direction of their lives and the lives of all those they care about.*

The central theme of many of my most powerful technologies is the skill of *flexibility*. In every human interaction, the person with the most options available to him or her will prevail! When flexibility goes hand in hand with the art of mastering change, you can create a life filled with ever-expanding levels of success, joy, and fulfillment. You'll discover not only who you truly are, but also everything you're capable of doing, thinking, and becoming.

For the past ten years, Nate has been one of my most trusted advocates in the essential skills of flexibility, anticipation, and adaptation. In *Thriving on Change* he has taken the science of change mastery to a new level. Here, set forth in accessible, easy-to-understand terms, are the philosophies and strategies that will not only immediately minimize the level of stress you experience on a daily basis, but will allow you to create the *momentum* and *quality results* you deserve in your life.

The first half of this book reveals the depth and breadth of the changes currently affecting our society, and the beliefs, strategies, and principles that you will need to master any change you encounter. The second half will lead you step by step through the secrets of change mastery, giving you everything you need to know in order to succeed—mentally, emotionally, financially, and spiritually—now and in the next millennium.

I have often said it's in our moments of decision that our destiny is shaped. To begin the process of change this very instant, all you must do is *decide* it's not enough anymore to live in "catch-up" mode, reacting to the stresses and strains of our rapidly shifting world. Instead, *get excited* about the tremendous wealth of opportunity available to those who are bold and resourceful enough to turn it to their advantage. Take your first steps now by following the expert guidance of my good friend, Dr. Nate Booth, in this remarkable new guide to navigating the waters of change in the 21st century.

Don't wait another minute longer—the journey begins now!

Anthony Robbins
Author, *Awaken the Giant Within* and *Unlimited Power*

Introduction

In the 1800s, the British army faced a change. For the first time, they were confronted with a crude yet effective machine gun. At that time, British battle strategy was to have their soldiers (who were wearing brightly colored uniforms) attack the enemy by walking toward them in long, straight rows.

As you might imagine, that kind of strategy made it easy for the enemy's machine gun to mow down the British troops. In their initial confrontation with the machine gun, five hundred British soldiers were killed or seriously injured in a matter of minutes! When the British field commander saw the devastation, he sent the following communication back to headquarters: "Send me five hundred more men!"

You would be amazed how many people and companies are approaching change today in the same way the British commander did then. They're using yesterday's solutions to cope with today's challenges, and it's not working. They're a perfect example of the classic definition of insanity—doing the same thing over and over again, expecting a different result.

Today, we must not only manage change, we must *thrive* on it. Unlike that long-ago British commander, we must be able to take whatever the world throws at us (at whatever speed it is thrown) and use it to our advantage. We must become Change Masters in every area of our lives.

That's what this book is all about—creating alternatives to "five hundred more men!"

If you're like me (and like most people living in this second half of the twentieth century), your life has been a series of constant and profound changes both personally and professionally. Yet perhaps, like me, you grew up in a time that didn't change nearly as fast as today's world, a time that didn't prepare us for the rapid change occurring on all fronts! Perhaps you too grew up in an area of the country that is a little (and sometimes a lot) resistant to change. My hometown of Harlan, Iowa (population 5,000) was your typical small Midwestern community. When I recall Harlan, I think of tree-lined streets . . . numerous churches . . . a town square with the courthouse in the middle and small businesses around it . . . high school football games at Merrill Field on Friday evenings . . . playing "kick the can" on warm summer nights . . . friendly neighbors (they'd do almost anything to help you) living in big old wooden houses . . . and the nine-hole golf course I rode my bike to most summer days.

I also recall the principles, moral values, and habits that are directly and indirectly taught in towns like Harlan. I will be eternally grateful I grew up in a place where all the things that should never change (community pride, hard work, contribution, honesty, fairness, integrity, team spirit) were a way of life. I've lived in other, more financially affluent communities, but none have been as rich in the truly important things as my hometown.

When it came time to decide what profession I wanted to follow, I looked around Harlan. Through my sixteen-year-old eyes I noticed a certain group of people who drove Buicks and lived in nicer homes. They had status and prestige; they got to play golf on Wednesday afternoons. These people were dentists, and so I decided to study dentistry. I would have been a physician, but they kept getting called off the golf course for emergencies!

I was married at eighteen (talk about change!) and went to the University of Nebraska, where I earned my D.D.S. degree in 1971. After graduation, we moved to St. Johnsbury, Vermont, where I built a very successful dental practice. However, after a few years I discovered I absolutely hated the drilling, filling, and billing of dentistry. So I made another huge change—I sold my practice, moved to Omaha, and earned a master's degree in counseling in 1983. I never wanted to use my counseling degree to help "troubled" people get back to halfway normal. Instead, I wanted to work with people like you, people who are already doing well and want to do better consistently.

In 1986 I began working for Anthony Robbins and his company, Robbins Research International, Inc., traveling from city to city selling tickets to Tony's live programs. I moved to San Diego in 1989 to take charge of training for Robbins Research's franchise division. With Tony's increasing popularity, more and more corporations and associations began asking for training from our company, and I decided that's what I wanted to do. So in 1991, I did my first corporate training program, for Honeywell Computers. Now I get to travel the world, sharing skills that improve businesses and lives. In my role as head corporate trainer for the Anthony Robbins Companies, I've conducted hundreds of training programs for corporations such as Arthur Andersen, AT&T, Eastman Kodak, IBM, Kraft Foods, Marriott International, NASA, Prudential Insurance, and Saturn Corporation.

In addition to these changes in my professional life, I've had numerous changes in my personal life. These include a second marriage to a wonderful woman with an eight-year-old daughter from a previous marriage, and my other two children going off to college.

As you can see, change mastery has been my personal and professional focus for the past thirteen years! I've met thousands of the best and brightest people, and, as is usually the case, they have simultaneously been my teachers as well as my students. I discovered that some people and companies were thriving on the changes happening around them; both their personal lives and businesses were enhanced as a result of change. I was intrigued to see *which* changes they embraced, and *how* they harnessed the power of those changes. I also discovered that other people and companies were being left behind by change, and the quality of their lives and business decreased as a result. I learned from them, too—I learned what *didn't* work (which is valuable information).

This book is the distillation of everything I've learned from my forty-nine years of personal and professional life experiences. I've compressed years of my own and other people's valuable experiences into knowledge you can absorb in the relatively short time it takes you to read and digest this book. What you hold in your hands is not a series of abstract theories about change. It is a collection of powerful *change utilization skills* you can apply immediately to your personal and professional life.

In these pages, you'll find everything you need to know not only to thrive on the changes that continually occur in your life, but also to be an *active creator of positive change* for yourself, your business, and your community. Each section is designed to help you shift your attitudes about change and give you specific, concrete, easy-to-use techniques you can use immediately to improve your life.

In Section One, "The Future Isn't What It Used to Be," you'll learn the basics of change utilization. In Chapter 1, you'll learn why change mastery is such a critical life skill. You'll also learn the six approaches people adopt when dealing with change. In Chapter 2, you'll learn why changes are occurring so rapidly in today's world. You'll also understand why I believe that you as a person and the world in general will be better and happier as a result of rapid change.

Section Two covers "The Four Cornerstones of Success in a Changing World"—principles, habits, beliefs, and strategies. Chapter 3 will show you how to create a rock-solid foundation for your life, a foundation built with the bricks of universal principles and habits you never want to change. In Chapter 4, you'll learn the power of belief to determine how well you utilize change. Then in Chapter 5, you'll learn the Six Thriving-on-Change Beliefs which Change Masters adopt in order to harness the power of change. Chapter 6 reveals the four strategies you can use to make improvements in your life: modeling, plussing, innovation, and reinvention. Finally, in Chapters 7 and 8, you'll learn how to stay in a resourceful emotional state as you travel through your changing world.

In Section Three, "Your Ultimate Change-Utilization Strategies" (Chapters 9 through 14), you will learn the specific skills you need to effectively react to, anticipate, create, and lead change. And in Section Four, "Your Place in the New Millenium" (Chapters 15 and 16), you'll learn how to take everything you've learned in the first fourteen chapters to soar into your future!

To get the most out of this book, it's absolutely vital that you begin to put these change utilization skills into action *today*, so you can more fully create the life you desire and deserve.

I'm sure you've noticed that the subtitle of this book is *The Art of Using Change to Your Advantage*. To me, the word *your* is not selfish. It is composed of two smaller words—*you* and *our.* In the final analysis, when you learn to use change to your advantage, our whole world improves!

I also believe that learning to thrive on change is too important to be treated seriously! That's why I've included cartoons throughout this book and kept the writing style informal and conversational. Enjoy your journey through this book—it will be great practice for your journey through our rapidly changing world.

I hope you're intrigued with what you've read so far, and I hope you're beginning to see that the same set of skills that worked well for you yesterday may not work tomorrow. I hope you see that shouting "Send me five hundred more men!" isn't the way to success. So turn to Section One right now to begin your journey to change mastery!

The Future Isn't
What It Used to Be

Have you ever felt that the world is changing so fast there's absolutely no way you can keep up with it? The pace of change has increased so dramatically over the past twenty years that we're in danger of feeling continuously overwhelmed. Just to give you a few examples:

- Of all the jobs that will be available in ten years, at least 50% haven't been invented yet.

- In the United States between 1987 and 1991, Fortune 500 companies reduced their number of employees by 2.4 million. In that same time span, small businesses (companies consisting of twenty or fewer employees) *added* 4.4 million employees.

- The information supply available to you doubles every five years.

- If you're under twenty-five years of age, you will change jobs every four years and careers every ten years.

- The largest private sector employer in the U.S. isn't AT&T, General Motors, or General Electric. It's Manpower Inc.— a temporary agency.

- Per dollar invested, computer power doubles every eighteen months.

- In 1980, 2% of the population in the U.S. was over the age of eighty-five. In 2050, 19% will be.

- A 1995 Chevrolet has more computer power in it than the Apollo 13 spaceship did.

- During the 1980s, 230 companies disappeared from the Fortune 500 list of largest U.S. corporations.

- Less than half of the work force in the industrialized world will be holding conventional full-time jobs in the year 2000.

The future isn't what it used to be! That's a fact. *What isn't a fact yet is how all this external change is going to affect you.* In your rapidly changing world, are you going to stick your head in the sand and pretend that change isn't happening? Are you going to sit back and just watch the changing world go by? Or are you going to learn to use change to your advantage? Will you be able to anticipate change and ride its waves to a better life? Will you become someone who actually creates change, a leader in the next millennium? The choices are yours—and these choices will determine your life path and your enjoyment of the journey!

You've probably noticed there are a number of books and seminars that teach you how to "cope" with change. Coping with change is certainly better than not coping, but there is another level of skill beyond that. It's what I call *change mastery:* the ability to utilize the power of change to improve your personal and professional life.

After twenty years of studying the effects of change on people, I've discovered most individuals fall into one of two categories:

1. Copers

Copers haven't discovered the immense power inherent in change. They . . .

- just "put up with" change,

- don't thrust ahead in our rapidly changing world,

- don't create passion and purpose in their lives,

- don't make the world a better place to live.

2. Change Masters

Change Masters thrive on change and use it to their advantage. Change Masters *harness* the tremendous energy change creates, and direct it so that they, their families, their businesses, their communities, and the world all benefit. Change Masters *utilize* change to create the future they desire and deserve!

That's exactly what this book will do for you. It will give you the specific tools you need to use change to your advantage. Armed with these tools, you will be able to approach your future with confidence and competence!

So take a trip down the path of change mastery by reading Chapter 1. The rapidly changing world is here! Now is the time to move beyond merely coping with change, and harness the vast potential around you.

Read on to discover how . . .

The Times, They Are a-Changin'!

The Times, They Are a-Changin'

My good friend Bob Weiland knows about life changes. Bob stepped on a booby-trapped 82-mm mortar in Vietnam when he was on his way to rescue a fellow soldier. He says, "My legs went one direction. The rest of my body went another!"

After he was found and taken to the hospital, Bob lay unconscious for five days. Because of his fighting spirit, he was rehabilitated physically and out of the hospital in six weeks. But then he sat around focusing on his limitations and problems, and his life was going nowhere as a result. One day he *changed:* He started to focus on resources and solutions. He told himself, "I still have what's really important. I have my mind, my spirit, and my connection with my Creator. I can become a model of possibility for other Vietnam vets. I'm going to walk across the United States on my hands!"

Bob started at Knott's Berry Farm in Orange County, California on September 8, 1982 and finished in Washington, D.C. on May 14, 1986—a journey of four years, eight months, and six days; 2,784 miles; and 4,900,016 "steps." His quest ended at the Vietnam Memorial, wall 22, line 47. Carved into the black granite on line 47 was the name *Jerome Lubeno*, the man Bob was going to rescue when he stepped on the mortar.

Many miracles occurred on Bob's journey. For example, when he was walking through a small town in Missouri, the person who had rescued him via helicopter in Vietnam and who now lived in that town

heard about Bob's journey and came to meet him again, this time
under better circumstances. Of all the routes Bob could have taken
across the U.S., he just "happened" to choose that one.

After his epic journey, Bob went on to break the world record in
the bench press for his weight class and to compete in several marathons
in his wheelchair. Today, he is happily married and continues to be a
shining example for others, sharing his story around the world.

Bob Weiland did more than cope with a huge change in his
life. He used change to improve as a person and to make the world a
better place for all of us. If Bob can do it with a change like that, we
can all do it with the myriad of smaller changes in our lives.

Bob demonstrates one of the essential secrets to utilizing change
successfully: **The meaning we attach to an event determines our
reaction to it.** Incredible as it may seem, Bob attached an empowering
meaning to having his legs blown off. This completely changed how
he felt about the situation, what he did in response to the situation,
and the results he got in life.

What meanings have *you* attached to the changes in your life?
Take a few moments to complete the following series of questions. They
are designed to help you examine the changes you've experienced in your
world and how you have reacted to them, positively and negatively.
You may want to record your answers in a journal or on a sheet of paper.

QUESTION 1:

What changes have I experienced in the following areas of my life?

List all the changes you can remember having an impact on
you for the last five years. Use the additional questions on the next
few pages to stimulate your memory and thought processes. Write
down everything you feel has had an effect on your life, both positive
and negative, because sometimes the smallest and most seemingly
insignificant changes can create the most upset or joy.

PERSONAL

What transitions have you experienced in your *personal life*? Did you meet the love of your life? Have you gotten married or divorced? Have you had a child? Have you lost someone you loved? Has someone moved in or moved out? Were any of these changes at your instigation, or did you feel they were imposed upon you from the outside? Would you say your personal life is better or worse than it was five years ago?

In the area of your *physical body*, is your health better or worse than it was five years ago? How? Have you or a loved one experienced a life-threatening situation or disease? Have you lost or gained weight? Have you taken charge of a particular area of your health, perhaps with exercise or nutrition? Do you feel you are in control of your health, or are forces outside of your control affecting it? How do you feel about the state of your physical body?

What transitions have you experienced in *your family* during the last five years? Have you or a child entered school or graduated? Have you moved to another house or community? Have you taken up or dropped a particular sport, hobby, or community activity? If so, what has been the result? How have you reacted to the changes in your family? Are you happy about the changes, or have they caused you pain? Has the quality of your family life improved or deteriorated over the last few years?

PROFESSIONAL

How has your *professional life* changed in the last five years? Have you changed jobs, been promoted, or been laid off? Have you changed careers or professions? Was it your choice, or was it due to necessity? Looking back on your choices, do you feel grateful or regretful? What would you have done differently, and why?

How do you feel about your *current occupation*? Are you fulfilled in your work? Do you feel you are making a contribution, or is it just a paycheck? Is there something you'd rather do? What's stopping you from creating the career of your dreams? And if your current occupation is exactly what you've always wanted, what's the downside and the upside? What's the greatest thing about what you do, and what's the worst? How much of your identity is linked to what you do? If you didn't have your current occupation, how would you define yourself? How does your current occupation make you feel?

Has *your company* made any major changes in the last five years, and how have they affected you? Has there been a turnover in the people you work with? Have you changed bosses or subordinates? Have there been any upheavals in your company or your industry? Do you feel you can control your own destiny in your company or industry, or are you at the mercy of outside forces beyond your control? Are you optimistic or pessimistic about your professional future?

What have you done to keep *your professional skills* current? Have you taken a course or gotten a degree, become computer literate, improved your communications or teambuilding skills? Do you want to start, or have you already started, your own business? How are you handling the constant changes of your professional life? Are you in control of your success, or are there factors that have stopped you—or could stop you in the future? How do you feel about the changes in your professional life for the last five years?

COMMUNITY AND WORLD

What changes have taken place among *your friends and extended family*, and how have you been affected? What changes have you seen in your town, city, neighborhood, state, church group, or social club, and how have these changes impacted you? Do you feel your community is better or worse than it was five years ago? Do you even feel you belong to any community at all—and if, so what does it consist of?

As you look at the world now as compared to five years ago, do you believe things are getting better or worse? How have the changes in *the world at large* affected you and your family? Do you feel you can do anything to help the world change for the better, or is it all too big a job for just one person? How important is your individual experience in creating a better quality of life for the future? How do you see the world five years from now? Are you optimistic or pessimistic about the future of your children and grandchildren?

Having examined the changes you've experienced in several areas of your life, answer these questions.

- To what degree am I participating in the changes around me?
- How much change do I actively create, and how much just happens to me?
- How optimistic or pessimistic am I about the changes in my life?

Finally, answer the following.

QUESTION 2:

What meaning can I draw from the changes occurring in my world today, and how does this make me feel?

Be perfectly honest—there's no need to be "politically correct." Take a look at your answers to the questions on the previous pages, and review the changes you've experienced in your personal and professional lives, in your family, in your community, and in your world. Notice especially how you reacted to these changes, and how you felt about the changes in your life. Have you felt overwhelmed at times by the extent and speed of the changes you've experienced? Has your life seemed a little boring sometimes because there hasn't been enough change? Have there been times where you wanted to change but were prevented by outside circumstances, or just couldn't get up the courage to make the leap?

Looking back over everything, what kind of statement would you make about the changes you've experienced, and how have they made you feel? Would you say something like, "Change is great and I love the newness of every day"? Or "I've been on a roller coaster of change and I just want things to settle down"? Or would your answer be something in between? Right now, come up with an answer two or three sentences long, and write it in your journal or on a sheet of paper.

Now analyze your answer on a scale of –10 to +10, with –10 being extremely negative, 0 being neutral, and +10 being extremely positive. Where does your answer fall? Write your evaluation in your journal or on a sheet of paper.

Extremely Negative										Neutral									Extremely Positive	
–10	–9	–8	–7	–6	–5	–4	–3	–2	–1	0	+1	+2	+3	+4	+5	+6	+7	+8	+9	+10

On a scale of –10 to +10, with –10 being "I'm a victim of change. There's nothing I can do about it," 0 being neutral, and +10 being "I'm an active participant in the change process," where does your answer fall? Write your evaluation in your journal or on a sheet of paper.

Victim										Neutral									Active Participant	
–10	–9	–8	–7	–6	–5	–4	–3	–2	–1	0	+1	+2	+3	+4	+5	+6	+7	+8	+9	+10

You'd be amazed at the variety of answers I get when people do this exercise. Their answers vary from, "The world is completely falling apart, and I can't do anything about it," to "This is the greatest time ever to be alive, and I'm an active player in the process!"

Your answers to these questions reveal your *beliefs* about change, which direct your *view* of your changing world, determine how you *feel* and what you *do* in response to change, and set in motion the *results* you ultimately get. An empowering set of beliefs is at the core of change mastery, and throughout this book, we'll show you how to develop the empowering beliefs you need to actively thrive on change. That's a big claim to make, but it's based upon my experience of coaching thousands of people over the past thirteen years.

I've done this exercise with thousands of people, and I've learned that those who thrive on change rarely evaluate their answers as +10. Instead, their answers tend to fall in the +4 to +8 range. But don't be concerned if you rated one or both of your answers lower than that. By the time you complete this book, you will have the beliefs and skills you need to be more optimistic and resourceful in mastering the changes you encounter!

The purpose of this book is not to tell you the precise actions you need to take in your changing world. Only you know where you are now and where you want to go in life. However, this book *will* give you an effective blueprint and a set of powerful tools to take your life from where it is right now and use the stimulus of constant change to create a masterpiece—a life that is enjoyable, exciting, and rewarding.

So let's get started!

Thriving On Change—The Basics

The essence of change mastery can be described in two sentences:

- Even in changing times, there is a set of principles and habits you never want to change. When things change, you must remain solid in your application of the great truths of life.

  AND . . .

- In changing times, the same set of beliefs and strategies that has gotten you where you are now will not get you where you want to go. When things change, you must change!

He that will not apply new remedies
must expect new evils.

SIR FRANCIS BACON

To thrive on change, you must be firm in your adherence to the principles and habits that form the core of a life well-lived while being flexible in the beliefs you hold and the strategies you employ to move ahead. Change Masters know when and where to be firm and when and where to be flexible. Throughout this book, you'll have the opportunity to learn and adopt the same beliefs, principles, habits, and strategies that enable Change Masters to ride the waves of change skillfully and with joy.

But before we can discover and appreciate what Change Masters do, we need to understand just what sets them apart from others. That's why I've identified the six fundamental ways people use to deal with the changes they encounter in their lives. Each approach has its use in different contexts; however, I think you'll find some approaches more useful than others!

THE SIX APPROACHES TO CHANGE

1. **Avoidance**
2. **Resistance**
3. **Apathy**
4. **Reaction**
5. **Anticipation**
6. **Creation**

1. AVOIDANCE

"I ignore change.
I have no idea what's happening."

Avoidant people don't even look at the external changes in their lives. They agree with a statement by Ogden Nash: "Progress may have been all right once, but it's gone on way too long." Avoiders isolate themselves from the world and let life pass them by. Using downhill skiing as a metaphor, avoidant people have their heads in the snow, refusing to recognize that skiing even exists!

The Encyclopedia Britannica company is a graphic example of the "head in the snow" approach to change. In 1993, they had their most profitable year ever, but by 1995 they were bankrupt. Why? They continued to sell only printed encyclopedias, ignoring a little thing called CD-ROM technology. They went from the top of their industry to bankruptcy in less than two years because they didn't adjust to the change in technology.

2. RESISTANCE

"I fight change!
It shouldn't be happening!"

Resistant people struggle
against change and usually get
upset in the process. In the
world of downhill skiing,
they're the ones trying to
ski up the mountain—all the
while complaining how hard
it is, how long it's taking, and
how all those other skiers are
going the "wrong" way!

People who resist change usually create an enormous amount
of pain for themselves and the people around them. Think about all
the workers in the last ten years who have resisted using computers
or adopting new technology on the job. Trying to resist change is like
standing in front of a steamroller that's going 100 mph and demanding
it stop. It's unlikely you'll stop or even slow down the steamroller;
chances are you'll just get run over.

This is not to say we should automatically embrace all change;
there are some changes it may be necessary to resist. If your neighborhood started to decay because drug pushers were moving in, it would
be very necessary to resist that kind of change with everything you've
got! But it's important to make sure you're not just resisting change
because of stubbornness or fear or wanting to keep things the way
they are. And all too often resistant people just don't want to change
anything—period.

3. APATHY

"I sit and watch change.
It's happening, but I don't care."

Apathetic people either don't care about what's going on or feel helpless to do anything about it. They complain a lot and do little. They're the people who spend their time worrying about being employed instead of taking action to be employable. While sitting in comfortable chairs in the lodge, these people watch others ski on the mountain.

Unfortunately, they don't realize their comfortable chairs could soon be taken away!

An excellent example of the apathetic approach occurred in the 1970s and early 1980s, when lower cost, higher quality Japanese cars hit the American market. The North American car manufacturers merely watched this fundamental change happening in their industry, all the while complaining mightily about "unfair" competition. As a result, GM, Ford, and Chrysler almost went under. Remember reading about "the death of the American car industry" in the early 1980s?

4. REACTION

"I adjust to change.
It's happening out there
and I'm making reactive internal changes!"

Reactive people wait for
external change to occur,
then react by making
internal changes to
accommodate the
circumstances.
This means
they're always
one step behind.
These people ski
down the mountain
of life and react to all the changes on the slope (bumps, changes in
slope angle, snow texture) as they encounter them. You'll often find
them complaining about "those awful bumps" and wishing someone
else would make the slope smoother!

In the mid-1980s, the American car industry finally changed
from the apathetic approach to the reactive approach, and the Big
Three made sweeping internal changes in their processes and products. If they had reacted to change sooner, their loss of market share
wouldn't have been as large.

5. ANTICIPATION

"I expect and prepare for change.
I have a good idea what's going to happen,
and I'm making adjustments proactively."

Anticipatory people actively look into the future, use all their knowledge to make an informed guess about what's going to happen, and make proactive changes that will enable them to stay ahead of external change. These people ski down the mountain

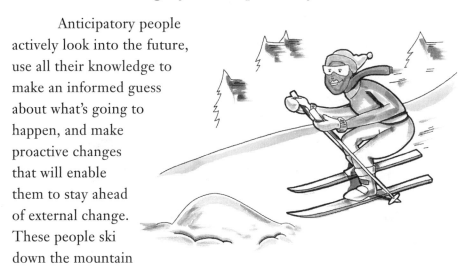

of life and anticipate changes in the slope ahead. They see a bump in the snow and use it to make a turn. They utilize the changes in the slope to their advantage!

In the late '80s, Packard Bell correctly anticipated both the explosive growth of the home computer market and the kind of stores where most buyers would purchase their personal computers (places like Sears, Circuit City, and Wal-Mart). They proactively created a line of attractively priced personal computers and developed close working relationships with major retailers. As a result, in the fourth quarter of 1994, Packard Bell was number one in U.S. personal computer sales, with an astonishing 55% share of the home computer market!

6. CREATION

*"I initiate change.
I use change to shape the world around me."*

Creative people make change happen, and then the world changes in response to them. All great leaders are change creators. They're like a skier with rocket power, jetting down the mountain far ahead of the rest, creating trails for others to follow! People like South Africa's Nelson Mandela, Microsoft's Bill Gates, and Mary Kay  Cosmetics' Mary Kay Ash have all created positive change, making the world a better place as a result. The Rubbermaid Corporation also knows the power of the creative approach—they introduced over 400 new consumer products in 1994. Rubbermaid's constant creativity is one of the reasons it has been at the top of its industry for many, many years.

Now let's analyze the different approaches to external change. The avoidant and apathetic approaches are passive. They may seem safe at the time, but in the long run they are the most dangerous of all because they lead to the world passing you by while you sit on the wooden bench of life, complaining about the splinters!

Think back to my friend Bob Weiland. What if he'd used the avoidant approach to change? A lot of people in his situation would have. They would have denied the impact of having to live without legs for the rest of their lives and ended up sitting in a VA hospital or at home, doing their best to distract themselves with TV, games, drugs, alcohol—anything to avoid the pain. Bob was stuck in the apathetic approach for a while. Right after he got out of the hospital he was so focused on his traumatic accident he sat around and did nothing. He realized the impact of the change but felt he couldn't do anything about it.

Faced with the choice between changing one's mind
and proving that there is no need to do so,
almost everyone gets busy on the proof.

JOHN KENNETH GALBRAITH

With the resistant approach, you are active but in the wrong direction. You're like a salmon swimming upstream, fighting the current with all your might. Unfortunately, this is not a strategy designed to help you utilize the positive changes occurring in your world. Why not apply the same amount of energy using the last three approaches to change? I guarantee you'll go much further much, much faster!

In the real world, you will need skills in each of the reactive, anticipatory, and creative approaches. There are going to be times when life will catch you by surprise and you will have to react to change. As much as possible, however, especially in the most important areas of your life you will want to *anticipate* key changes. And in other areas of your life you will want to *create* change so you can be a leader.

Bob Weiland has used all three of these approaches to transform his life. He finally decided to *react* to the change of being without legs by breaking out of his apathy. By deciding to focus on solutions instead of challenges, he began to *anticipate* how his life could be better with a shift in attitude. And finally, when he committed himself to becoming a model of possibility for other Vietnam vets by walking across the U.S. on his hands, he utilized the power of the *creative* approach to lead others.

As Bob will tell you, making these changes wasn't always easy. But "easy" isn't all it's cracked up to be! The challenge and zest in life comes from making the "hard" choices of knowing when and how to make reactive, anticipatory, and creative changes in your life. When you effectively use the strategies in this book to assist you, you'll be surprised how easy the hard choices can become.

You now have the basics for learning to use change to your advantage. Thriving on change appears simple, doesn't it? You may be saying, "Yeah, it's simple, but it's not necessarily easy to do in my 'real' world." That's why, at the end of each chapter, you'll see an "Exercises for Action" section. I recommend you write the answers in a journal or notebook so you can review them and refer to them as you read this book. As you develop new skills, think of applying them in these four areas of your life.

EXERCISES FOR ACTION

1. Take another look at the statistics on pages 2 and 3. In what ways could these changes affect your personal, professional, family, and community life? How are you preparing for the changes you're likely to experience in the next five to ten years? If you fail to prepare for changes like these, what could be the result? How could you take advantage of these kinds of changes in your future?

2. I'm sure you did the exercise on pages 8–12. If you didn't, go back and do it now. It is important that you do this exercise now, because you will use your answers later.

3. Review the Six Approaches to Change (pages 15–20).

   A. When in your life (if ever) have you used the avoidant approach to change? What did you try to avoid, and what were the consequences of that decision? How would things have been better if you had chosen to take action?

   B. When in your life (if ever) have you used the resistant approach? What change did you try to fight, even though you knew it was inevitable or perhaps even beneficial? How could you have handled the situation differently? Could your life have been better as a result of your choosing another way to deal with this change?

   C. Where in your life (if ever) have you used the apathetic approach to change? What were the consequences of believing you couldn't do anything about the situation? What action could you have taken that would have changed the situation completely? And how would your life have been improved as a result?

D. Where in your life do you need to react to a specific change you believe is coming (or is already here)? List two or three examples, and write in your journal how you plan to handle these changes successfully.

E. Where in your life would you like to do a better job of anticipating change? In your journal, list two or three situations where it's critical for you to anticipate upcoming changes and take action today to prepare for change tomorrow.

F. Where in your life do you want to do a better job of creating change? List at least three areas where you're committed to being the director of your own destiny and how you will create the change necessary to shape your life for the better.

There's no doubt that change is happening faster, it's coming from more directions, and it's affecting more areas of your life now. The next chapter will reveal the following.

- You are already superbly equipped to utilize this change.

- You and your business have all the resources you need to thrive in a rapidly changing and competitive marketplace.

- You can help our world come through these changing times and provide a better life for everyone!

Read on to discover . . .

A Worldwide Change for the Better!

CHAPTER 2

A Worldwide Change for the Better

Rapid change is occurring in every corner of the world. (Have you looked at the most recent maps of Eastern Europe, Asia, and Africa?) This became especially clear to me when I conducted a series of training programs in Malaysia in 1994. I was amazed at the degree of change occurring right before my eyes! Malaysia is moving from an agriculturally based economy to a more balanced (and global) system. Motorola, Intel, National Semiconductor, and other multinational corporations have built or are building huge assembly plants in Malaysia. As I write, the tallest building in the world is being constructed not in New York, Tokyo, or London, but in Kuala Lumpur, Malaysia's capital. Across the street from my modern hotel in Penang was a beautifully restored mansion that had been turned into a Kentucky Fried Chicken restaurant!

Now, I don't believe all change is "good" or that there won't be some short-term pain for certain groups of people along the bumpy road of change. But I do believe that, in the long run, the majority of changes occurring in the world today will be beneficial to most people. It's our responsibility to share the knowledge and beliefs that will help others take advantage of this global climate of change.

Is all this change a new phenomenon? Definitely not. Since the beginning of time, change has been a constant in our world. What has varied is

- how widespread the change is (pervasiveness),
- how fast the change occurs (pace),
- how the change affects our lifestyles (quality).

Let's take a look at these factors one at a time.

PERVASIVENESS

It's only been in the past one hundred years or so that technology has advanced to the point where different cultures around the globe can communicate change reliably and quickly. It's reached the point today that news of any significant change is spread around the world almost instantaneously. This has created a rapid increase in the pervasiveness of change.

PACE

Change is definitely happening more rapidly in almost every part of our world. The fact that the information supply available to you doubles every five years is strong evidence of this increased speed. You're probably feeling the pressure of this increased pace of change in your own life. In fact, it may be why you're reading this book!

QUALITY

What rightly concerns most people is whether all this global and rapid change is making our planet a better place to live. I believe the greatness of any society is based upon its ability to change for the better—to use change as a tool for growth. I'm optimistic that, as a global village, we can and will do just that.

To understand how we can use change to our advantage, let's first take a look at four causes of rapid worldwide change.

Four Causes of Rapid Worldwide Change

1. **Rapid improvements in technology**
2. **Instantaneous worldwide communication**
3. **Intense global competition**
4. **Changing demographics and psychographics**

1. **Rapid Improvements in Technology**

   With new technology, quality can be improved, costs can be reduced, and often fewer people are needed to do the work. Today, with the same number of workers, U.S. manufacturers produce five times as many goods as they did at the end of World War II.

   Here are just a few examples of the effects of rapidly improving technology:

   - Recently I was videotaping a commercial at a local TV station here in San Diego. The three robotic cameras in front of me were controlled by one person in the control booth. There were no traditional camera operators anywhere on the set!

- Using advanced technology, IBM Credit Corporation can now process a new credit application in four hours instead of the six days it used to take. Even more amazing, 5% fewer claims processors can now process one hundred times the number of applications.

- When you buy Procter & Gamble's disposable diapers at a Wal-Mart store, the checkout scanner records the sale, orders another box of diapers from the warehouse, and requests that a credit be sent to Procter & Gamble.

- New technology in product development has led to rapid expansion in the number of products available, as well as dramatic improvements in the products you buy. Think of the enormous industry created by the development of the personal computer. In 1994 and 1995, sales of computers alone (not including software sales) increased by 20% each year. And the products are getting better and better. I recently read that the 1994 Minolta 9xi camera has more intelligence than a 1982 Apple® II computer.

2. Instantaneous Worldwide Communication

It all started with the live worldwide broadcast of the Muhammad Ali–Joe Frazier boxing match in Manila in 1974, a little over twenty years ago. (Do you remember "The Thrilla in Manila?") Now it's come to the point where we broadcast wars live. In the 1991 Persian Gulf War, the cameras were waiting on the beach when the Marines landed in Kuwait!

Rapid communication not only spreads change more quickly, it's the catalyst that ignites the innovative spirit in those who can utilize the technology. For example, if you have a Metropolitan Life insurance policy, your claim may be processed in an office in Ireland. The people of Harlan, Iowa, my home town (population 5,000), process subscriptions for numerous magazines that are published in cities across the country.

Rapid communication has also changed where we live. If you have a computer, a modem, and a fax machine, you can live in places like Bend, Oregon, Madison, Wisconsin, or Charleston, South Carolina, and still conduct business with people half a world (and several time zones) away.

3. Intense Global Competition

At the end of World War II, the United States was winning the global economic war by default. The economies of most of the industrialized world, including Germany, Italy, Japan, France, and England, were devastated. In addition, after the deprivations of five years of war or more, there was a huge demand for consumer goods at the same time there was a limited supply. So people bought whatever was available, regardless of quality. Their expectations were low because whatever they bought was better than what they could (or couldn't) get during the war years. That began to change in the '60s and '70s when high-quality consumer products came from all points on the globe. Due to this overabundance of products, consumers began to demand higher quality at a competitive price. The trend has continued into the '90s. Every day, it seems, you can buy a better product for the same or less money than you could two years ago. This is especially true in high-tech areas such as computers, computer accessories, appliances, and consumer electronics. What's more, due to ever-increasing worldwide competition, the trend of higher quality for lower prices can be seen in everything from candy to clothing, sports equipment to toys, etc.

4. Changing Demographics and Psychographics

Demographics refer to the age, income, education, sex, and other social characteristics of a population; psychographics refer to the opinions, values, and emotions that drive behavior. There have been dramatic changes in both areas over the past forty years.

Demographics

North America's demographics have been greatly impacted by the Baby Boomers, those people who were born between the late 1940s and mid-1960s. This huge population is a driving force in the world economy. In the '50s they needed more grade schools. In the '60s they needed more high schools. In the '70s new colleges were popping up all over the place. Now the Boomers are moving into their peak spending years, and our economy is going to boom right along with them. Harry Dent's fascinating book, *The Great Boom Ahead*, details the effect Baby Boomers have had and will have on the world economy as they age.

Psychographics

Psychographics—the opinions, values, and emotions that drive behavior—are the prime determinants of lifestyle. The best and smartest companies use psychographics to create and market products that people perceive will enhance their lifestyles. For example, does Nike just sell running shoes? Not a chance. Like all successful companies, Nike is in the lifestyle business, and they market shoes for the physically-fit lifestyle millions of people desire.

Unlike their World War II–"Bob Hope generation" parents, Baby Boomers have a lifestyle that is more accepting of change. The Boomers are in their thirties to late forties now, and are taking control of politics (Bill and Hillary Clinton, Newt Gingrich, and Al and Tipper Gore, for example) and corporations (Bill Gates at Microsoft,

Phil Knight at Nike, and Anita Roddick at The Body Shop). The psychographics of Baby Boomers have been and will continue to be one of the primary determinants of world opinion and economics for a long time to come.

Now that you know why change is happening so rapidly, let's move on to why I am (and you should be) optimistic about the future.

Six Reasons to be Optimistic About the Future

1. **A history of change**
2. **Cultural diversity**
3. **An increase in the number of democratic governments and free-market economies worldwide**
4. **Multiple and abundant resources**
5. **A booming economy**
6. **The basic goodness of humanity**

1. A History of Change

All countries have different histories of dealing with change. The United States, Canada, and Australia, for example, experienced mega-change in a relatively short period of history (less than two hundred years). Today, most of the population of these countries are descended from immigrants who made one of the greatest changes imaginable—leaving their homelands behind and giving up everything to come to a new land.

In many other countries where the way of life remained
unchanged for centuries, the change rate has only begun
to accelerate rapidly in the past twenty-five years. Malaysia
is an excellent example of a country where decades of
progress have been made in just a few short years.

Regardless of whether or not your society is accustomed to
change, today the world is experiencing the most potent
and pervasive shift since the Industrial Revolution over
two hundred years ago. At that time, the world economy
changed from an agricultural base to a manufacturing base,
and millions of people moved from farms to cities to
work in factories. The changes occurring in today's
Communication Revolution are as sweeping as the
changes of the Industrial Revolution.

2. Cultural Diversity

While the degree of cultural diversity varies from country
to country, it's increasing almost everywhere. This vibrant
and ever-changing melting pot of cultures is the perfect
caldron for change. How's this for cultural diversity in
action: In 1994, U.S. consumers bought more taco sauce
than ketchup!

3. An Increase in the Number of Democratic Governments and Free-Market Economies Worldwide

Change is much more likely to flourish in countries that
provide the freedom for change to occur. Look how quickly
the societies of many of the former Eastern Bloc countries
are changing, now that they are free to choose their own
form of government and shape their economies as they wish.

4. Multiple and Abundant Resources

In varying degrees, the world has the tools—the human resources, natural resources, educational systems, business and communication infrastructures, and technologies—to create rapid and life-enhancing change. How we preserve, allocate, and utilize these resources for the benefit of humanity is one of the greatest challenges and opportunities we face in the 21st century.

5. A Booming Economy

According to Harry Dent, the Baby Boomers' peak spending years will extend from 1993 to 2007. With the benefits of low interest rates, low inflation, and a maturing information technology, through the year 2007 the world will experience a booming economy, providing a fertile field in which rapid change can grow.

6. The Basic Goodness of Humanity

This is the most important reason I'm optimistic about our future. I believe that the basic goodness of humanity will, in most cases, cause us to use rapid change as a vehicle to create a better world. Yes, there will be bumps along the way. There will be some crazy twists and turns. We may run out of gas on occasion, and this basic human goodness will keep us on the road, focused on a better world for everyone.

Albert Einstein believed that the most important question you will ever answer is, "Is the world a friendly place?" My answer is, "Almost always, yes!" I believe the people in this "friendly place" will use change to create a future full of progress.

Now, let's apply the information in this chapter to your life by doing the Exercises for Action that begin on the following page. Remember, knowledge alone is potential. Knowledge put into action is power!

EXERCISES FOR ACTION

1. How have each of the four causes of rapid change affected your personal, business, family, and community life? List two or three ways in which you have experienced the impact of

    A. rapid improvements in technology,

    B. instantaneous worldwide communication,

    C. intense global competition,

    D. changing demographics and psychographics.

2. Explore your personal history of change. What major changes have you successfully made in your life so far in terms of residences, jobs, relationships, responsibilities, and personal interests?

3. What additional changes would you like to make in the next year, and how will they benefit your life, your family, and your community?

As you can see, I believe that change leads to progress. It's absolutely critical we base our progress on something that doesn't change—those principles and habits that are universally recognized as the foundation upon which all great lives and great civilizations are built.

Read on to discover the . . .

Four Cornerstones of Success in a Changing World!

Four Cornerstones
of Success in a
Changing World

S tatues have pedestals. Paintings have frames and canvasses. Cathedrals have foundations. Every lasting work of art has a structure that supports it through time. The same is true of your life in our rapidly changing world.

In this section, you will learn how The Four Cornerstones of Success—principles, habits, beliefs, and strategies—create the solid foundation to support your life as the winds of change swirl around you.

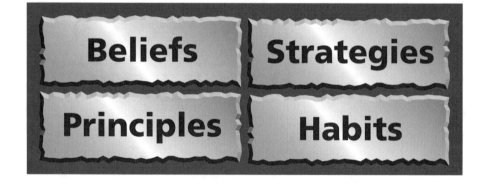

Principles and Habits: Your Rock-Solid Foundation

Principles | Habits

The great truths are too important to be new.

W. SOMERSET MAUGHAM

Back in Chapter 1, you learned that effective change utilization can be summed up in two sentences, the first of which is, "Even in changing times, there is a set of principles and habits you never want to change." The great truths W. Somerset Maugham describes above are the principles that govern human effectiveness at all times, especially in times of change. These universal principles are an important part of every society and have stood the test of time. They are rock solid. They can't be broken. To paraphrase Stephen R. Covey in his "must read" book, *The 7 Habits of Highly Effective People*, "We cannot break these principles. We can only break ourselves against these principles."

The great truths are self-evident. They're a part of our being—we just know they're right. These principles can be buried by life's experiences, but they will always pop up again. They can be pushed against, but they will always win in the end because they are right. They can be interpreted differently, but their power is not lost in the variety. They can be ignored for a time, but life will always give you a wake-up call.

These principles include

• honesty	• contribution
• growth	• dignity
• vitality	• love
• fairness	• service
• integrity	• quality
• respect	• teamwork

These principles act as the hull and keel of your ship on the ocean of life. They are mostly under the waterline, that is, not always apparent; yet they are the most important component of your ship. You can be an expert sailor, with the best navigational equipment, accurate maps, and perfectly trimmed sails, but you will not stay on course with a defective hull or keel. At best, the slightest change of wind will push you off course. At worst, your ship will sink in the storms.

I used to say, "I've heard all this stuff before," when people discussed the basic principles upon which they built their lives. I discounted the value of these principles because they're so obvious and simple. Then I realized I kept hearing them repeatedly because they were universally true! They are such a key ingredient of success, successful people can't help but mention them.

The trouble with Man is twofold.

He cannot learn truths which are too complicated;

and he forgets truths which are too simple.

REBECCA WEST

So how can you tell the difference between a principle and something else? Often it's easiest to begin by saying what principles are *not*.

Principles are not beliefs. Beliefs are human inventions based upon our experiences and what we've been told about the experiences of others. Principles are universally held and are independent of an individual's experience. The closer your beliefs match universal principles, the more accurate and useful they will be. In Chapter 5, you will learn the Six Thriving-on-Change Beliefs, all of which are founded upon universal principles.

Principles are not strategies. A strategy is a unique set of actions designed to achieve a specific outcome. Strategies are situation-specific: A strategy that works in one situation may not work in another. Excellent parents know this—they don't raise all their kids the same way. Great salespeople know this—they don't sell everyone the same way. Top coaches know this—they don't coach everyone the same way.

Because principles are fundamental truths that have universal applications, you can apply a single principle to various situations in your personal life, your business, your family, your community, and your world. The more your strategies are based upon universal principles, the more effective they will be. In Chapter 6, you will learn how to construct your strategies for success in a changing world.

Your Daily Habits Reveal Your Principles

Your daily habits are the best indicator of how well you've internalized universal principles. For example, if you've internalized the principle of honesty, you will develop the habit of telling the truth.

Let's take a look at some of these universal principles and see how closely your habits reflect them. Ask yourself the following questions.

- HONESTY—How many ways did I tell the truth today? Did I stand up for what I believe? Was I honest even if it was painful or inconvenient? Did I excuse myself for telling a "social" or "white" lie or for withholding information I knew should have been presented? How was I honest today with myself and others?

- SERVICE—Did I give excellent service to all my customers today? (Your customers include your teammates at work, your business customers, your family, and your friends.) How did I serve all those I encountered? How could I serve more?

- INTEGRITY—Did I do what I said I was going to do today? How did I keep my commitments to myself and others?

- CONTRIBUTION—How did I give to an individual or a group today, especially when I didn't have to? How did I make the world a better place to live today? How did I make people feel better and do better because of their association with me?

- GROWTH—Was I able to spend some time today in the process of self-improvement? Did I read, watch educational television or videotapes, or listen to educational or inspirational audiotapes? What did I do today to help myself grow? (You can count reading this book, you know!)

- VITALITY—How healthfully did I eat today? Did I exercise? Did I breathe deeply? Did I avoid foods and situations I know are not good for me?

What you are . . . *thunders*

so that I cannot hear what you say.

RALPH WALDO EMERSON

In their remarkable book, *Built to Last,* James Collins and Jerry Porras discuss the results of their study of the factors that contribute to the success of corporations through time. One critical factor they identified was what they called *"a strong core ideology,"* defined as the core values and purpose upon which the company was built. Companies with a clearly defined core ideology based on universal principles, effectively communicated in word and deed to all employees, were much more likely to succeed than similar companies in the same industry that lacked a strong core ideology. In other words, built-to-last companies and their employees succeeded in large measure because they built an empowering foundation of universal principles and the habits they created.

Collins and Porras tell a revealing story about one such built-to-last corporation, Merck & Co. At considerable expense, the pharmaceuticals company developed and gave away a drug called Mectizan that cured river blindness, a disease that infects over a million people in Third World countries. Merck also brought streptomycin to Japan after World War II, a time when tuberculosis was rampant. They did it in spite of the knowledge they wouldn't make any money off the deal.

Why does Merck have the habit of helping people when others don't? It has to! The habit of helping others is the natural result of internalizing the universal principles of *service* and *contribution*—two core values Merck has espoused since its founding. In 1935, long before mission statements became popular, George Merck II said, "[We] are workers who are genuinely inspired by the ideals of advancement of medical science, and of service to humanity." In 1991, fifty-five years later, Merck's chief executive, P. Roy Vagelos, echoed the same thought when he said, "Above all, let's remember that our business success means victory against disease and help to humankind."

Is it any wonder that Merck is rated by Fortune 500 CEOs as one of the most respected corporations in America? Or that Merck is consistently voted one of the best corporations to work for in the U.S.? Or that Merck is the largest pharmaceutics company in Japan today? The principles Merck & Co. lives by are clear in everything they do.

When our lives are based solidly upon unshakable, powerful principles, it's much easier to deal with any changes that might occur, because we know there are some things that never change.

Many authors, especially Stephen Covey, have done a splendid job describing the power of these universal principles to help you create a fulfilled life. It's absolutely critical that you have the foundation which universal principles provide.

How to Change a Negative Habit to a Positive One

Most people think changing a habit is a difficult and challenging process. After all, a habit is a behavior that's become entrenched, right? In reality, however, a habit is nothing but an action that's been repeated through time, a result of built-in cues that trigger the action and built-in rewards that reinforce the action.

The Habit Chain

CUE → ACTION → REWARD

I've discovered there are two steps people tend to go through when they successfully replace a negative habit with a positive one. First, they realize intellectually and emotionally that

1) the old, negative habit violates one or more universal principles—"The habit of stealing, even if it's taking paper clips from the office, just isn't right!" and/or

2) this particular habit isn't in the best long-term interest of themselves or someone they love—"My smoking isn't just shortening my own life, but could really be hurting my child, my spouse, etc.," and/or

3) the habit is at odds with their identity, their view of who they really are—"It's just not like me to be so undisciplined as to let myself get this flabby and out of shape!"

Second, they break the old, negative habit chain and replace it with a new, positive habit chain. Remember our diagram of how a habit is built:

The Habit Chain

There are two places where you can break the Habit Chain.

1. You can *remove the cue* or *radically change it to signal a different action*. If the smell of cigarette smoke on your clothes is a cue for you to crave a cigarette, you may want to get all your clothes cleaned to eliminate the odor. If going to a bar or having a drink was your cue to smoke, you may want to stop going to bars or drinking

for a short period of time, just until the connection between drinking and smoking is broken and a new connection established.

2. You can *remove the reward* and/or *create a punishment for taking the negative action*, then *create a reward for the new and improved action*. Every time you have a cigarette, you may want to force yourself to rub the smelly, old, stale cigarette butt all over your hands and face so all you or anyone else smells when you approach is dead cigarettes. Perhaps every time you elect not to smoke in situations where you would have done so before, you put $5 in a special fund for a vacation or massage or some other treat.

Let me give you an example of breaking a habit chain. Let's say you have a negative habit of watching a lot of useless TV when you're feeling bored at home. The cue is boredom. The action is watching TV, and the rewards are the positive feelings you receive from distracting yourself.

To successfully replace this negative action with a positive one, you first must intellectually and emotionally realize that the old habit isn't in your best interest and is at odds with your identity as an intelligent, learning person. Then you break the old, negative habit chain and replace it with a new, positive habit chain as follows:

(1) Remove the cue by doing interesting things in the evening so you won't feel bored; and/or change the meaning of the cue by making the feeling of boredom a trigger that you need to learn something—by reading a book or listening to an educational audio- or videotape, for example.

(2) Associate pain to the old habit by agreeing to pay your spouse $10 for every useless TV program you watch; likewise, associate pleasure for the new, positive habit by treating yourself to a massage after you've read three educational books.

Establishing a set of positive daily habits based upon universal principles is one of the most effective means to create a rock-solid foundation upon which to stand in our ever-changing world. With a strong set of principles and habits, the winds of change can blow all around you, and you can bend with the wind as needed—because you know your foundation is immovable!

Now it's time to apply the information in this chapter to your life by completing the Exercises for Action on the following pages. It's the most important component of this book!

EXERCISES FOR ACTION

Principles

1. Take a look at the list of universal principles on page 38. Which of these principles are currently active in your life? Write two examples of how you have demonstrated each currently-active principle in the last month.

2. Which principles would you like to experience more in your life? Choose two principles you would like to focus upon for the next thirty days. Write each in your journal, and next to it, write two ways you can apply this principle and the effect taking those actions will have upon you and those around you. For example:

Principle	Two Actions	Effect
Honesty	1. I will catch myself not keeping commitments to myself, and keep them.	1. I will be more disciplined and focused; I will be able to stick to my exercise program! I will feel better about myself.
	2. I will tell the truth when my boss asks my opinion of an idea I think is possibly harmful.	2. My boss will know I can be relied upon to say what I really think rather than just covering myself. If I tell the truth while still respecting the person who is presenting the idea, I will be able to raise the level of honesty of the entire team!

You may wish to create a list of universal principles and post them where you can see them every day—at your desk, on your refrigerator, etc. They will serve as a gentle reminder of the rock-solid foundation that will help you handle any change that comes your way!

Habits

1. List several of your good habits. On what principles are they based?

2. List a few of your bad habits. What universal principles do they violate? What's going to happen in your future if you keep these bad habits?

3. What good habits would you like to adopt instead, and on what principles are they based? How will your life be better with these habits in place?

Remember, your principles—and the habits that support them—are the hull and keel of your ship. They keep you afloat in good weather and bad. They are constant. What isn't constant on the sea of life are the winds and currents you encounter on your journey—the beliefs and strategies you use to adapt to our ever-changing world. They come from different directions, at different velocities, at different times. When the winds or currents change, you need to change the set of your sails. Your beliefs are the best way to make the appropriate changes in your sails so that you can capture the maximum amount of wind to propel you quickly to your destination!

Read on to discover . . .

The Regenerative Power of Belief!

CHAPTER 4

The Regenerative Power of Belief

When I walked into the room, I knew who he was instantly. It wasn't his stature or his clothing; he was about five foot three and wore a nice, though not expensive, sport coat. But there was something about the way he stood, moved, and gestured that told me he was the one who had led his company, Investors Diversified Services (IDS), in sales that year. Quite an accomplishment out of thousands of financial planners! It's an even greater accomplishment when you realize Alex Alexander had been number one at IDS for forty-six out of the last forty-nine years.

You might think his success was due to factors such as education or training. Nope. He had a high school education and was a shoe salesman before he started with IDS. It wasn't exceptional product knowledge, and it certainly wasn't dashing good looks! As I listened to him speak about his fifty years in the business, I realized what it was: He was full of *empowering beliefs* that were based on universal principles! One after another, these beliefs kept rolling out of his mouth—beliefs about his products and services, beliefs about his company, beliefs about himself and why he was on the planet. From just one session, I wrote down thirty-four empowering beliefs that helped create his success, drive his behavior, and produce his amazing results.

Two of his key beliefs were:

1. "Everybody is a prospect. I can be of service to anyone."

2. "They're going to be glad we got together. Maybe my future clients aren't going to want to meet with me at first, but after they get to know me and see the services I provide, they're going to be glad we met."

Alexander told a story about making a sale to the CEO of a large corporation. On the way out of the building, he noticed the receptionist. Now, most financial planners believe, "Only certain people are prospects," and "People don't like to talk to financial planners." If you have those two beliefs in your head and you walk by the receptionist, what do you do? You keep right on walking! And the scary part is, you don't even have to think about it. It's the "natural" thing to do. On the other hand, if you believe, "Everybody is a prospect," and "People are going to be glad we got together," what do you do when you notice the receptionist? You stop and talk to him or her! Do you have to force yourself to do it? No—it happens naturally.

With Alex's set of beliefs, he stopped, talked to the receptionist, and made a small sale to the woman. Two years later she married a senior vice-president of the corporation. Alex continued to be the couple's financial advisor and earned some nice commissions in the process. All because of his empowering beliefs!

When you really think about it, you realize your current beliefs didn't just come out of thin air. You weren't given them at birth. They were *choices* you made at various points in your life. To thrive on change, the beliefs you choose must be based upon unalterable principles that will keep you on course no matter what. These beliefs have tremendous power to enhance your ability to create the future you desire. Undoubtedly, these beliefs must be modified continually as you adapt to your ever-changing world.

In Chapter 1, you learned, "Even in changing times, there is a set of principles and habits you never want to change." You also learned, "In changing times, the same set of beliefs and strategies that has gotten you where you are now will not get you where you want to go!"

In this chapter, you will learn how your beliefs act as the ignition switch to start a cycle of events that will drive you closer to or farther away from your goals. In the next chapter, you will learn the Six Thriving-on-Change Beliefs that are the most powerful igniters of success in a changing world!

So, let's begin to explore the power of belief. Take a moment to come up with the words you'd use in the following sentences. Use one word for each blank. You may want to write the sentences (including your words) in your journal.

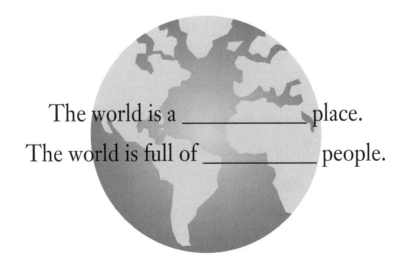

The world is a _____ place.
The world is full of _____ people.

Intrigued? We'll be examining your answers to these questions a little later, but meanwhile, let's see how beliefs affect the way we experience the world.

The Belief Cycle

Beliefs are so powerful because they set into motion a six-step cycle. What you believe determines

1. what events you *focus* on in your world,

2. what the events *mean*,

3. how you respond to the events *emotionally*,

4. what *action(s)* you take,

5. what *result(s)* you get,

6. which then reinforce(s) your *belief*.

To see the belief cycle in action, let's use the example of one of the world's greatest inventors, Thomas Edison. As you know, the first practical light bulb was only one of his hundreds of inventions. One of Edison's key beliefs was, "There is no such thing as failure. I learn something from every experiment I do." With this belief, let's suppose Edison just completed an experiment that didn't work out the way he intended.

1. **What did he *focus* on?** He focused on what he learned from the experiment. Edison believed there was something to be learned from every experiment, regardless of the outcome, that would aid him in his next effort.

2. **What did the event *mean* to him?** Instead of thinking, "I failed *again*," Edison would say, "I just learned another way *not* to invent the light bulb. This experiment just brings me one step closer to my goal."

3. **How did he respond to the event *emotionally*?** Did he pout in a corner? Did he go to the refrigerator and eat? Did he get depressed and pop a Prozac? No, he got excited instead, because he believed he was one step closer to his goal.

4. **What *action(s)* did he take?** He conducted another experiment!

5. **What *result(s)* did he get?** He invented the light bulb. After how many separate experiments? Over ten thousand!

6. What did this result do? **It reinforced his *belief*,** "There is no such thing as failure." And he went on to invent the phonograph, the first motion picture, and many other marvels.

Edison's belief was the first step in a cycle creating the emotions, actions, and results that made him a success. His beliefs shaped him as a person. Right now, your beliefs about the world and the people in it are shaping you as a person, too!

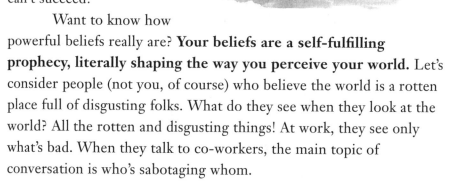

Have you ever been "on a roll"? What happens? You *believe* you can accomplish great things. You *focus* on all the reasons why you will succeed. You create empowering *meanings* from everything you encounter. You have positive *emotions* which drive your resourceful *actions*. These lead to great *results*, and your brain says, "Hey, I'm good!" which strengthens your *belief,* and the cycle continues.

Conversely, have you ever been "in a rut"? What happens? You don't *believe* you can accomplish something. You *focus* on all the reasons why you won't succeed. You lack empowering *meaning* in your life. You have negative *emotions* which produce *inaction* or the wrong actions. These lead to lousy *results*, and your brain says, "See, I told you that you couldn't do it!" which strengthens your *belief* you can't succeed!

Want to know how powerful beliefs really are? **Your beliefs are a self-fulfilling prophecy, literally shaping the way you perceive your world.** Let's consider people (not you, of course) who believe the world is a rotten place full of disgusting folks. What do they see when they look at the world? All the rotten and disgusting things! At work, they see only what's bad. When they talk to co-workers, the main topic of conversation is who's sabotaging whom.

At home, they watch the news on TV so they can see and hear all the rotten and disgusting things that happened in their community and around the world. Then they watch *COPS* so they can feel like they're riding in the police car as they chase terrible people. Finally, they switch to Ricki Lake so they can see and hear all the rotten and disgusting people "up close and personal."

How does this make them feel? Rotten and disgusted. What kinds of actions do they tend to take when they feel this way? Do they take any action at all, or do they just give up? What results do they get in their life? Rotten and disgusting ones. This reinforces their generalized belief that the world is a rotten place full of disgusting people. It's the self-fulfilling prophecy principle in action!

How does the belief cycle impact your life? Look at the two words you wrote in the blanks in the sentences, "The world is a _____ place" and "The world is full of _____ people." Now, in your your journal, write those same words in the following sentence:

"I am _____ and _____."

For example, if you wrote, "The world is a great place," and "The world is full of amazing people," you would write, "I am great and amazing." If, on the other hand, you wrote, "The world is a terrible place," and "The world is full of horrible people," you would write, "I am terrible and horrible."

What were your answers? I've done this exercise with thousands of people, and I'm always amazed at the correlation between what someone believes about other people and the world, and the cycle of focus, meaning, emotion, action, and results these two beliefs put into motion. I love to walk around the room and see the answers people invariably write. Those who seem to radiate pain or discomfort in one form or another have negative words such as "awful," "disgusting," "sick," "lousy," and "bad" written in the blanks. Their beliefs about the world and people direct their focus to the negative in life, creating negative meanings, negative emotions, negative actions, and negative results, which all reinforce their negative beliefs.

In contrast, people who exude love and joy, who have risen to the top of their organization or who have created a flourishing company from scratch, have written positive words such as "exciting," "wonderful," "fascinating," "unique," and "beautiful" in the blanks. Their beliefs about the world and people direct their focus to the positive in life, creating positive meanings, positive emotions, positive actions, and positive results, which all reinforce their positive beliefs.

When my friend Joe Kolezynski first had me do this exercise many years ago, I wrote, "The world is a funny place," and "The world is full of interesting people." He then pointed out that the two words people often use to describe me are "funny" and "interesting." When an event happens in my life, I routinely say, "That's funny," and "That's interesting." I tend to *focus* on funny and interesting things— I see them everywhere, which means that's the way my world is. I feel joyful and interested; I do funny and interesting things, which gives me fun-filled and interesting results in my life, which reinforces my belief that the world is a funny place full of interesting people. Do you see how belief jump-starts the cycle?

If the words you wrote in the blanks weren't very flattering, you may just be having a bad day—or maybe you should take a closer look at your beliefs about the world and the people in it. Your beliefs are a major factor in creating how you feel, what you do, and the results you get.

In reality, you "are" or "aren't" anything. If you wrote "disgusting" in your "I am _____ and _____ " sentence, for example, you aren't really disgusting. You may feel disgusted at times and do disgusting things every once in a while (and you may get some disgusting results), but you're not disgusting. Be very careful about what you say after the words, "I am," because you are taking on that word as a part of your identity. How much better will your life be if you identify with universal principles rather than the negative feelings we all have at times? What if every time you used the words, "I am," they were followed only with positive expressions? At the very least, if you happened to be in a negative mood, what if you expressed yourself using words like, "Right now I'm *feeling* _____ , but that's not who I really am"?

This may seem either like a small difference or too much like Pollyanna, but it will help you build an important habit—that of identifying with universal principles rather than transitory negative emotions. Try it for a week, and see how different your daily life can become!

Now, let's study another example of beliefs in action. Go back to the "What's the meaning of all the changes in the world today?" question you answered on page 12. **That meaning is created by your beliefs about change.** What are some of these beliefs? How do the resulting meanings support or hinder you? And what new, empowering beliefs/meanings could you put in their place?

Mental Creation First, Physical Creation Next

Belief is the backbone of the mental creation process, which is the first step toward creating any outcome you desire in life. The second step is physical creation. Let's discuss the two steps one at a time.

1. Mental creation comes first.

You must create the outcome you desire in your mind before you create it in the real world. A prime example of the power of mental creation was Walt Disney, who mastered what he called "imagineering." After Walt died, his brother Roy was in Orlando for the opening of Disney World. A reporter asked Roy, "Isn't it a shame that Walt never got to see this place?" Roy replied, "You're wrong. He saw it in his imagination before we ever built it. That's why you're seeing it today!"

In 1961 John F. Kennedy went out on a limb by emphatically stating on television that by the end of the decade the United States would put a man on the moon and bring him back alive. President Kennedy got an entire nation to believe him; we created the outcome mentally long before we did it physically in 1969.

When Martin Luther King, Jr. proclaimed in 1963, "I have a dream," he described that dream in detail in the present tense. Dr. King knew the dream (the mental creation) had to precede the physical reality. He enlisted millions of people to believe in his dream and take the necessary action to make it real.

A rock pile ceases to be a rock pile
the moment a single man contemplates it,
bearing within him the image of a cathedral.

ANTOINE DE SAINT-EXUPÉRY

A dream is an outcome that has purpose and passion behind it. A clearly defined dream is the catalyst that mobilizes the resources for its achievement. In 1961, the resources we eventually used to get to the moon and back were not available. We discovered them on the way to the dream. Dr. King had a very clear outcome, but what he shared with us was his vision, not the steps along the way. He enthusiastically proclaimed, "I have a dream!" not, "I have a strategic plan." He knew the plan would be developed from the passion of the dream.

The foundation of mental creation is belief. I see this happening all the time in my life. When I have a new program I want to create, the information I need just seems to jump out of the woodwork. I'm sure the ideas were always there; I just didn't detect them until I had a specific outcome for their use.

The same is true with your dreams and aspirations. When you have a crystal-clear dream of what you want to be, do, have, and give in life, the resources that will help you create it will "magically" appear on the way to your dream. Don't wait to have everything you need before you start. It will rarely be there. Life will provide you with the means to achieve your dreams. You just need to tell life in no uncertain terms what you want, then move toward your desire with purpose and passion!

The empires of the future are the empires of the mind.

SIR WINSTON CHURCHILL

---

2. Physical creation is the next step.

President Kennedy took action and led a nation on a historic journey. Dr. King put his dream into action and influenced millions of people to do the same. Yet physical creation is the step where most people fall down. They may have a dream, but they don't follow through in an effective and sustained way. They lose their dream through inaction. After enough inaction, internal mental creation also stops because the brain says, "What the heck— you never do anything with my ideas! I'm shutting down!"

Even if you're on the right track,
you'll get run over if you just sit there!

WILL ROGERS

Chapter 6 will show you how to create the most effective strategies to put your dreams into action. But if you don't have the belief and the dream first, all the strategies in the world won't get you where you want to go. As Wayne Dyer and many other authors have said, "You'll see it when you believe it!"

In the next chapter, you will learn the six beliefs Change Masters use to turn their mental creations into physical reality. Now, let's apply the principles in this chapter to your life by doing the Exercises for Action on the following pages.

EXERCISES FOR ACTION

1. Identify a belief you have in your life right now that limits you, something that stops you from making the changes that would improve your life. Examples: "I start great, but I never follow through;" "I'm too (old, young, poor, stupid) to succeed;" "I don't have the (time, money, resources, intelligence, background) to go for what I really want;" "I never get the breaks;" "Getting what you want isn't supposed to be easy;" etc. Come up with the belief that has stopped you in the past, and write it in your journal.

2. Using the belief cycle, notice the impact of holding that belief. Answer the following questions.

   A. How has this belief directed your *focus?*

   B. How has this belief caused you to create unresourceful *meanings* in your life?

   C. How do you *feel* as a result of holding this belief?

   D. How have your *actions* been shaped by this belief?

   E. What have your *results* been with this belief?

3. You now have the opportunity to change this belief into one that will empower you rather than limit you! What would be a belief that is the antidote—the opposite—for the belief in #1? Examples:

Old Belief	New Belief
I start great, but I never follow through.	I keep building a little more every day, and my results accumulate steadily to create the life I want!
I'm too (old, young, poor, stupid) to succeed.	I have all the resources I need inside of me to move ahead. I'll discover any additional resources I need along the way. Other people who were (older, younger, poorer, less intelligent) than I have succeeded, and so can I!
I don't have the (time, money, resources, intelligence, background) to go for what I really want.	If I really want it, I can get anything I go for. It's just a question of learning and allocating my resources effectively.
I never get the breaks.	I create my own opportunities!
Getting what I want isn't supposed to be easy.	When I know what I want, every step along the way can be enjoyable and effortless!

Write your old belief and your new antidote in your journal.

4. Now, run your new belief through the Belief Cycle, and jot down any changes you notice. Make sure you really *associate*—that is, feel emotionally as well as understand intellectually—the consequences of adopting this new belief.

   A. How will this belief direct your *focus?*

   B. How will this belief cause you to create resourceful *meanings* in your life?

   C. How will you *feel* as a result of holding this belief?

   D. How will your *actions* be shaped by this belief?

   E. What will your *results* be with this belief?

5. Write this new belief down and post it where you will see it constantly. Make a point of noticing how this belief is affirmed by experiences in your life. And enjoy your new empowering belief!

6. Your last exercise is to recognize the power of mental creation in your own life. Take two minutes to write down everything you currently are, have, or do, that was once just a dream or idea. Include possessions, jobs, relationships, achievements (like college degrees or recognitions), etc. Everything from making the Little League team to finding the person of your dreams to buying just the right plant for your desk is fair game. Remember, virtually everything we encounter in the world was once just an idea in someone's head. Make your own mental creation list now!

An empowering set of beliefs that ignite you to thrive on change is crucial as you move into the 21st century. You have the power to choose your beliefs now. The $64,000 question is, "Which beliefs are the most effective ones to hold?"

That's exactly what you will learn in the next chapter, as you discover . . .

Six Thriving-on-Change Beliefs!

CHAPTER 5

Six Thriving-on-Change Beliefs

Beliefs

In the last chapter, you learned the power of beliefs to shape how you feel, what you do, and the results you get in your changing world. In this chapter, you will learn the six specific beliefs on which Change Masters thrive.

I identified these beliefs by conducting hundreds of interviews with successful people, reading books, listening to audiotapes, and reading newspaper and magazine articles. There were six beliefs these people held in common, beliefs that came up again and again. They are some of the most powerful tools you can use to thrive on change in our rapidly changing world.

BELIEF #1:

Change equals opportunity.

This is the primary belief of all Change Masters. Whenever they experience a change in their personal lives or businesses, they immediately think, "What are the opportunities here?"

Rapid change is creating greater opportunities for more people and companies than ever before. Rapid change levels the playing field because it demands intelligent, quick, unique anticipation, and reaction. People and companies who are smart, flexible, and quick will consistently and unhesitatingly run up and down the newly level playing field, enjoyably scoring multiple touchdowns. People and companies who aren't smart, flexible, and quick will be left in the dust!

Here are some examples of how change levels the playing field and creates tremendous opportunities for those who are ready.

- The Great Depression of the 1930s was definitely a change in the American economic condition. While there were huge numbers of people who experienced great financial hardship, more people became millionaires in the U.S. during the Great Depression than almost any other period in our history. Times of challenge can also be times of tremendous growth for anyone who looks for and seizes opportunity.

- The computer industry has changed more rapidly than almost any other field. In 1985, Beny Alagem bought the rights to the name *Packard Bell*, a defunct consumer products company that had made radios in the 1920s and televisions in the 1950s. Alagem tailor-made computers for the expanding home computer markets, distributed his products through non-computer retail outlets like Sears and Wal-Mart, and cornered a large share of the market. In just under six months, from October 1994 to March

1995, Packard Bell sold more personal computers than any other company! Alagem was able to turn Packard Bell into the success it is today because he knew change equals opportunity.

- In the year 2000, women-owned small businesses will generate more new jobs than all the Fortune 500 companies combined. Change equals opportunity for women, minorities, and many other people who in the past have been excluded from traditional power structures.

- Between 1987 and 1992, not only did 143 companies disappear from the Fortune 500 list, but 143 more took their place. Change created opportunity for companies that were smart, flexible, and quick.

- In 1995, Coca-Cola sold more products in Japan than any other U.S. company. Who do you think was number two? It was Amway, one of the oldest and best-known network marketing companies. The world of retailing is changing rapidly in today's global marketplace.

The winners of tomorrow will deal proactively with chaos and will look at chaos per se as the source of market advantage, not as a problem to be got around.

TOM PETERS

Employ Change Utilization Belief #1 daily. When you experience a change in your life or in your business, say, "Hallelujah! There is tremendous opportunity nearby waiting to be discovered!" Then look for the opportunity that awaits you.

BELIEF #2:

When things change, I must change!

All Change Masters believe they must change when the world changes, not the other way around. They are prepared to change their beliefs and strategies to take advantage of what is happening. Yet they never abandon the universal principles and habits by which they live.

Did you have an Aunt Millie when you were growing up? She started out as an excellent schoolteacher for five years. Then she got tired of teaching and moved on to real estate. She did well for six years, got tired of it, became a successful financial planner. Now she runs her own small business offering financial services to professionals. She has a staff of seven and is president of the local Financial Planners' Association.

Fifteen years ago, what did we call the Aunt Millies of the world? Undependable, unstable job-hoppers. They were people who "couldn't decide what they wanted to be when they grew up."

You probably also had an Uncle Mel in your family. Mel worked long and hard for the same company in the same kind of position for forty-four years. What did we call the Uncle Mels of the world fifteen years ago? Dependable, solid, respectable.

Things have definitely changed today. The Aunt Millies of the world are becoming more and more widespread, and are highly valued in the work force. The Uncle Mels are becoming relics with limited employability. Aunt Millie was a Change Master. Uncle Mel was not. Millie knew, "When things change, I must change!" Mel never learned that lesson.

Flexibility and adaptability are required characteristics in the work force today. For example, Dell Computer is one of the top five personal computer companies because it is far more flexible than its competitors. Dell sales representatives talk to and take orders from thousands of customers each day. Through them, the company learns firsthand any changes in consumers' buying patterns. Using this information, Dell can then make internal production adjustments on a daily basis. Incidentally, Michael Dell started the company from his dorm room at the University of Texas. Talk about change leveling the playing field!

The Walt Disney Company has faithfully preserved its purpose of "using imagination to bring happiness to millions," yet it also has continually changed its product strategy—from short cartoons, to feature length cartoons, to feature films, to television programs like *The Mickey Mouse Club* and *The Wonderful World of Disney*, to theme parks, to videos. The change in strategy has continued with Disney's acquisition of one of the "Big Three" television networks, Capital Cities/ABC, in August 1995.

When I do training programs, I ask the audience, "On a scale of one to ten, how important is flexibility in today's world?" The answer is a resounding "Ten!" the vast majority of the time. Flexibility is the one word that sums up Belief #2—"When things change, I must change!"

The significant problems we face cannot be solved

by the same level of thinking we used

when we created them.

ALBERT EINSTEIN

BELIEF #3:

There is always a way to use change to my advantage.

Change Masters are creatively stubborn. They believe there is *always* a way to utilize change to their advantage!

As you may have noticed, I'm a huge fan of Walt Disney. Walt knew there was always a way. Those who worked closely with him learned very quickly never to tell Walt, "This can't be done." That statement simply didn't compute in Walt's mind. His experienced co-workers always said, "Well, Walt, this might be difficult because . . ."

Thomas Edison knew there was always a way. He kept looking, learning, and doing until he achieved the result he desired. You need to do the same thing when change occurs in your life. You need to find a way to use change to your advantage. That silly little saying, "When life gives you lemons, make lemonade," is more important than you know. When life gives you a "problem," if you use the problem to learn and grow you'll be unstoppable.

I do this all the time when I'm speaking to groups. Some of the weirdest things happen in front of an audience. If the microphone starts screeching, I can either stand there and complain about the sound system, or I can use the problem to my advantage by saying, "Those of you who have teenagers will be used to this!" It's gotten to the point now that I welcome unexpected changes in my training programs because I know I can use them to add humor to the situation or as a way to illustrate a point I'm making.

Never give in, never give in, never, never, never, never.

SIR WINSTON CHURCHILL

BELIEF #4:

I'm going to enjoy my journey through this rapidly changing world.

Change Masters make it a priority not only to utilize change to help them get to their dreams, but also to enjoy the journey along the way. Here's a powerful example of an entire company that's enjoying the journey. In the highly competitive and rapidly changing airline industry, one company consistently stands above the crowd— Southwest Airlines. Anyone who has flown Southwest knows that its employees definitely enjoy the journey! They wear shorts or slacks, knit shirts, sneakers, and smiles. They use their sense of humor to turn flights into an enjoyable experience.

I was on a Southwest flight about two years ago. As the passenger in front of me opened the overhead compartment, a flight attendant stuck her head out and shouted, "BOO!" I haven't seen that on Delta in a while! On another flight, the man in front of me was hobbling on board the plane with a badly broken leg. He was in a cast from his thigh all the way down to his ankle. The flight attendant took one look at him and said, "Looks like you've been flying America West!"

On most airplanes, the preflight instructions are so boring I will do almost anything to distract myself. Not on Southwest! They turn it into a comedy routine with bits such as "There are fifty ways to leave your lover, but only six ways to get out of this airplane," or "For those of you who haven't been in a car since 1962, here's how you work your seatbelt," or "If you smoke in one of our lavatories, we're going to kick in the door, hose you down with a fire extinguisher, put you out on the wing, and show you the movie *Gone With the Wind!*"

The ultimate Southwest experience is flying into Las Vegas on a Friday afternoon or evening. It's like being in Times Square on New Year's Eve! On a recent Vegas trip, even the pilot got into the spirit. Just before we pulled away from the gate, he announced, "Cowabunga, dudes! We're going to back this crate out of here and boogie on over to Vegas!" The crowd went wild. High fives were happening up and down the aisle. The minute the wheels touched down in Vegas, the passengers went nuts, spontaneously applauding and yelling.

On the same flight, a flight attendant announced the following just before we deplaned: "We have a very special person on board tonight—he's celebrating his 100th birthday. We would really appreciate it if you would congratulate this person when you see him. So, on the way out of the plane please say Happy Birthday to your pilot!"

The fun-loving attitude at Southwest was put into motion by its founder and CEO, Herb Kelleher. He made "a sense of humor" a top criterion for hiring new employees at Southwest. At one time Southwest required pilot applicants to take off their pants or skirts and wear Southwest Airline shorts with their jackets during the job interview! Herb Kelleher himself has been known to hop on a flight dressed as a big white bunny rabbit, just to liven things up. He also helps out the baggage handlers at the terminals on busy days. Herb loves his employees, and they love him. On his last birthday, they took out a full-page ad in *USA Today* saying, "Happy birthday, Herb! Thanks again for making Southwest such a fun place to work!"

Herb Kelleher enjoys the journey through his rapidly changing world. So do his teammates at Southwest, and so do the passengers on their planes. The result? Southwest usually has the highest customer satisfaction rating in the business.

I think laughter may be a form of courage.

LINDA ELLERBEE

I do training programs for dozens of corporations each year. I enjoy comparing the "fun level" of the group with how well the corporation is doing financially. In almost every case, there's a definite correlation: Companies who are having fun are doing well financially. Now here's my question to you: Are these companies having fun because they're doing well financially, or are they doing well financially because they're having fun? The answer is, YES! It's a continuous cycle of fun and success that enjoyably carries these corporations toward their visions and goals.

BELIEF #5:

There is a life lesson to be learned from every change in my life.

Remember the old *Candid Camera* TV series? Occasionally people would begin to figure out that they were being fooled and ask, "Am I on *Candid Camera?*" You need to do the same kind of thing when a change occurs in your life, except your question should be, "What's the life lesson I need to learn from this change?" It's as if God or Life or Mother Nature (however you want to view it) teaches you valuable life lessons using the changes that are intentionally placed in your path. It's up to you to determine what that lesson is and learn from it by responding appropriately.

Lessons come from both "good" changes and "bad" changes; you usually won't know which is which until you're further down the path. I had an interesting change happen to me about three years ago. I was doing a five-day intensive training program for a corporation that had brought in people from all around the country. My programs are always very high energy from beginning to end. This training started at eight in the morning and finished at ten at night, and I also went to lunch and dinner with the group. At the end of each day, I answered questions for thirty minutes, then went home and spent an hour or two preparing for the next day's session.

On the morning of the fourth day, I couldn't get out of bed. My body just wouldn't cooperate. Luckily, I was at home in San Diego, so my wife Dawn literally hauled me out of bed and threw me into the shower. That's when I asked myself, "What's the lesson here?" Not being able to get out of bed was the change I had to deal with. What was the lesson I needed to learn? Slow down and don't do the training with so much intensity? Don't go at it for as many hours each day? Have someone help me? I decided that the lesson I needed to learn was, "I'm not in good enough shape. I should be able to do almost anything for a week!" At the time, I was working out two or three days a week for thirty to forty minutes a session. I increased my workout to ninety minutes five or six times a week, with aerobic exercise and strength training. Now I can easily handle the exertion of a five-day training program.

Right now, think of a time in your life when something really "bad" happened to you. As you look back on it today, with all the learning you've accumulated since that time, wasn't it one of the things that helped positively shape you into the person you are today? It only seemed "bad" at the time. Life just gave you another valuable lesson, and will keep giving it to you until you learn it!

Who decides what the lesson is for each change in your life? You do! You can either choose a lesson that makes you feel helpless, one that causes you to assume the worst about other human beings, or you can choose a lesson that will move you ahead in life, one that helps you become a better person. Right now, think of a change you once experienced when you didn't choose to learn a lesson that moved you forward. For example, you ended a relationship with your lover. The lesson you chose was, "That person is a jerk! In fact, everyone I get into a relationship with is just out to use me. I'm never going to commit myself to another person—it's just not worth it." Will that lesson help or hinder you in having another romantic relationship in your life?

What would happen if you changed the lesson to something like this? "Both of us made mistakes in our relationship. I realize now that the mistakes I made were A, B, and C. I see that now, and I'm not going to make the same mistakes again. I'm going to grow from this. Also, I learned that I value certain qualities in a lover, which are D, E, and F. I'm going to look for those qualities in the people I meet. Now that I think about it, I already know someone who has those qualities—Pat. I think I'll give Pat a call!"

You have the ability to choose the lesson you wish to learn—one that keeps you stuck or moves you backwards, or one that intelligently moves you forward to experience all that life has to offer. Choose your lessons wisely and well!

If we chose what was going to happen to us,

we would never grow!

MARK SANBORN

BELIEF #6:

I'm an active participant in the change process!

People respond to change more resourcefully when they believe they are active participants in the change process. There are two parts to Belief #6:

Part A — **Communication.** You must know what's going on.

Part B — **Control.** You must believe you have some control over how events are affecting you.

If Part A is missing, you're uninformed—and what you don't know *can* hurt you. If Part B is missing, you feel helpless. Numerous studies have shown that feelings of helplessness cause people either to shut down or to resist change actively or passively. I realize there are times when you can't control the external changes in your life. But you can always control the way you *respond* to change, both in how you feel (emotions) and what you do (behaviors).

It's especially important to make people active participants in the change process when you're leading group change. Two of the cardinal management sins I see in corporations are 1) the failure to communicate effectively with employees about the nature and amount of the external change the company is facing; and 2) the failure to involve employees in planning and executing the corporate response to change. In Chapter 14, you will learn more about leading group change effectively.

SIX THRIVING-ON-CHANGE BELIEFS

1. Change equals opportunity.
2. When things change, I must change!
3. There is always a way to use change to my advantage.
4. I'm going to enjoy my journey through this rapidly changing world.
5. There is a life lesson to be learned from every change in my life.
6. I'm an active participant in the change process!

Now that you know the Six Thriving-on-Change Beliefs, you can create a plan to utilize any external change that occurs in your life. I call this the Change Utilization Planner.

Change Utilization Planner

First, identify one *external* change you're facing in your personal life or your business. Then answer the following questions.

1. **What opportunities could this external change create for me (us)?** Take five to ten minutes to list as many possibilities as you can. If you're on a team, let the whole team brainstorm ideas.

2. **How do I (we) need to alter the way I (we) think or the way I (we) do things in response to this change?** Be specific here. List all the possible ways that you and/or your group will have to alter your thinking and behavior in response to the external change.

3. **What are the life lessons I (we) need to learn from this?** Be more general here. Life lessons are basic principles that affect many areas. Some examples of life lessons include increased flexibility, improved communication, and greater caring.

4. **What can I (we) do right now to become a more active participant(s) in the change process?** Get very specific about the actions you're committed to taking. Be sure you remember communication and control.

Here are two examples of the Change Utilization Planner in action, one with a personal change, one with a group change. A man I'll call Mark had just been laid off from his job as an account executive at a large advertising company. He was unsure what to do next, so I suggested he use the Change Utilization Planner to make the most of this transition. Here are his answers.

1. What opportunities could this external change create for me?

"Well, first this gets me out of the nine-to-five (or in my case, the nine-to-nine) office grind. I've been working such long hours for so many years, I haven't really explored the other opportunities out there. I can actually take some time now to look around for other career options.

"This also gives me the chance to relocate to a different part of the country. I've been thinking it would be great to live in the Pacific Northwest. Hey! I may even be able to start up my own company in a small town somewhere, and get out of the big city rat race I've been stuck in since college.

"I could also completely change career directions. I've always wanted to do more with my graphic arts degree, and I've really gotten into computers over the last five years. My friend Sam has been working with a company that creates pages for the World Wide Web. That would be a different way to use my advertising experience and at the same time take a whole new direction, one that's only going to grow enormously in the foreseeable future. Besides, it would be fun! This is great—there are at least ten other careers and directions I could take right now. And I'm still young enough to pursue them!"

2. How do I need to alter the way I think or the way I do things in response to this change?

"I need to plan my financial future very carefully. I got a good severance package from my company—they're giving me two months with pay to look for another position—and I can get unemployment benefits if my job search takes longer than that. But I need to make sure I have money set aside to take care of my needs, and I've got to have a plan for the most likely contingencies. Also, I need to meet with the company's human resources director to talk about health benefits and how to handle the money I've invested in the company pension plan.

"Second, I have to start looking at myself as not just an 'advertising account executive,' but as someone with a unique set of marketable skills that can fit into many different industries and job descriptions. I don't want to look only in my field; I want to expand my career horizons, and this is the perfect opportunity to do that.

"Third, I've got to make sure I regard this as a positive change, a new beginning. I've seen a lot of other people who have been laid off really get depressed and blame themselves. My boss told me my work wasn't the problem, it was just the downsizing of the entire company that forced the department to eliminate two-thirds of its people. Still, I'm going to watch my internal self-talk, to make sure I'm not beating up on myself. I'm also going to make sure I get great references from my boss and the vice-president of the division!

"Last, I'm going to contact all the clients I personally deal with to let them know what happened in as positive a way as possible, and to assure them that their new account executive will continue to take great care of them. I want to support the company through this tough time, and who knows? One of my clients might provide me with a great lead for a new position!"

3. What are the life lessons I need to learn from this?

"I need to learn to be flexible and anticipate change. I need to learn there are a lot of people who are on my team and are ready to support me. It's been great to see how many of my clients, family, and friends have rallied around me and offered me assistance without any kind of pity or blame.

"Also, I need to learn to create more balance in my life. I spent so much time at work for the last few years that I've let my level of fitness slide, and I've neglected my kids. I need to learn that it's not about me, that there are factors over which we have no control, but I can always control how I feel and how I respond to what happens. I need to learn to plan for the worst and expect the best."

4. What can I do right now to become a more active participant in the change process?

"I'm going to make an appointment with Human Resources today to get totally clear on my severance package and all my options. I'm going to call Sam about his computer company. I'm going to send away for information on at least three communities in the Pacific Northwest. I'm going to make a list of all my past and present clients and set up a schedule to contact each of them individually. I'm going to ask my boss for a recommendation right now. And tonight, I'm going to leave work at five and take a long walk with my kids!"

In the second example of using the Change Utilization Planner for a group change, Mark's boss, Martha, has to deal with losing two-thirds of the people in her department. She is expected to pull her team together and not only manage all the clients on their current roster but also actively pursue new business, regardless of her diminished personnel resources. Here are her answers to the Change Utilization Planner questions.

1. **What opportunities could this external change create for us?**

   "Well, we are absolutely not going to be able to do things the same old way ever again! In order to take care of our existing clients and bring in new business, we're going to have to look at everything we do in a whole new light. Each member of the team is going to have to take on new responsibilities and rely on each other more than ever. We used to be a department of individuals who took care of certain accounts. We can't do it that way anymore—there's too much to do with too few people. We're going to have to create a much higher level of real teamwork.

   "Plus, when Steve [the VP in charge of the department] told me about the layoffs, he said I would have a free hand to use whatever creative ways I could come up with to get new business. All I had to do is to produce the results, he said; the methods were up to me and my team. I've had a lot of ideas about ways to pursue new business that I've never been able to put into place before. I'm going to get the whole team involved in brainstorming how to get new clients!"

2. **How do we need to alter the way we think or the way we do things in response to this change?**

   "We have to totally change the way we think and what we do to get results. We have to get out of the old 'account executive' mode and into the 'account team' concept. We have to completely revamp how we handle accounts, from contacting potential customers to producing the final product. And I have to make sure the entire team feels supported as part of this re-engineering process. This has been an emotional time for them, seeing so many of their colleagues leave. I want them to feel they are an integral part of making this department work and that I'm not looking to work them to death to make up for the people who are gone. This is about working smarter, not harder!"

3. What are the life lessons we need to learn from this?

"We're going to have to rely on ourselves to bring in the business the company needs to prosper. We can't just depend upon client referrals anymore; we're going to have to be much more proactive. We're also going to have to learn flexibility. Everyone on the team should know how to do everyone else's job—and be ready to do it, too! We're going to have to be strong and courageous as we tackle this new opportunity, and we need to support each other completely. And we're going to have to be very honest with each other. One of the roughest parts of this whole thing was that I didn't know how big the reorganization was going to be until the very last moment. I've committed to my team that I will inform them immediately of every management decision which might affect them. As far as I'm concerned, they're as much a part of the management team as I am, and I will absolutely include them in all decisions, as well as let them know our results. We're all accountable."

4. What can we do right now to become more active participants in the change process?

"It's important to make sure that everyone who's leaving is taken care of, emotionally and financially, and that the team can say their goodbyes in as constructive a manner as possible. I'm going to set up interviews with each person in the department, both the people who are leaving and those who are staying, to clear up any bad feelings and/or possible misunderstandings.

"Then, we're going to have an off-site departmental meeting to launch this new era. I want to make sure everyone knows this is the time to get out all their bad feelings and, more important, to bring all their ideas to the table about how to make this department work. Maybe we'll do one of those ropes courses that are designed to build teamwork and promote creativity! By the end of the meeting, we should have a clear plan for handling all our old accounts and creating new clients, using the resources we have.

"I'm also going to set up a schedule for contacting all of our current clients personally, to assure them that this transition will not affect the high level of service they've come to expect from us. If their account executive is leaving, I'll arrange to visit each client and introduce their new account executive in person. One of our team's first assignments is going to be to come up with some way to re-solidify our relations with current clients, before we start pursuing new business.

"Next, I'm going to set up a meeting with Steve to let him know how we're planning to re-engineer the team. Just because he's been less than communicative with me doesn't mean I have to be the same way with him. I'm going to do my best to enroll him as an active supporter of our new, revitalized department!"

I've helped hundreds of groups use the Change Utilization Planner in their companies. You would be amazed at the resourceful answers they create in only twenty minutes. Being a Change Master doesn't take long if you use this planner as a guide.

The next time an external change occurs in your life or business, use the Change Utilization Planner as a quick way to discover how you can use this change to your advantage.

The Six Thriving-on-Change Beliefs you learned in this chapter are powerful triggers that ignite a more powerful belief cycle and move you rapidly toward your dreams. How much more change mastery would you have if you embraced them now?

Let's apply the information you learned in this chapter to your life by doing the Exercises for Action that begin on the next page.

EXERCISES FOR ACTION

1. Identify one external change you're facing in your personal life. Run that change through the Change Utilization Planner by answering the following questions.

   A. What opportunities could this external change create for me (us)?

   B. How do I (we) need to alter the way I (we) think or the way I (we) do things in response to this change?

   C. What are the life lessons I (we) need to learn from this?

   D. What can I (we) do right now to become a more active participant(s) in the change process?

2. Identify one external change you're facing as part of a group. This can be your business, your family, or any other group. Run that change through the Change Utilization Planner by answering the questions below.

   A. What opportunities could this external change create for me (us)?

   B. How do I (we) need to alter the way I (we) think or the way I (we) do things in response to this change?

   C. What are the life lessons I (we) need to learn from this?

   D. What can I (we) do right now to become a more active participant(s) in the change process?

Back in Chapter 1, you learned that the same set of beliefs and strategies that has gotten you where you are now will not get you where you want to go. In the last two chapters you've learned about the transformational power of belief and the Six Thriving-on-Change Beliefs.

These beliefs will give you the confidence you need to use change to your advantage. However, this is only half of the solution. In order to thrive on change, you must feel both confident and competent—taking appropriate action.

Read on to discover your . . .

Strategies for Success!

CHAPTER 6

Strategies for Success

The year was 1985. We were taking a fifteen-minute break in the middle of a four-hour training program I was doing for an agency that sold Mutual of Omaha insurance. It was the first corporate training I had ever done. My contact came over to me and whispered, "Nate, why don't you cut it short and give us only twenty more minutes? The sales agents are threatening to leave because you're so boring." He tried to be nice, but the message was clear.

I wasn't surprised he said what he did because he was right. My material was good, but I didn't know how to present it in an interesting way. I was dedicated to doing a good job, but I didn't know how to do it. I didn't use the right *strategy*. The definition of strategy in this context is "a unique set of actions designed to achieve a specific outcome."

My second corporate training program was for IBM. (I like starting with the little guys!) Five minutes before I was to begin, I went to the restroom and, to make a long story short, I couldn't get my zipper up! Now, when I feel tension, I sweat like crazy. So here I was in this IBM restroom, frantically hopping around, trying to get my zipper up and sweating like a maniac. I finally got the zipper up with a minute to spare, so I went to the sink to throw some cold water on my face in a last attempt to cool down. I had just bought a new burgundy silk necktie, because at that time almost all the men at IBM were wearing blue suits, white shirts, and burgundy ties. I bent over the sink and—you guessed it—my tie fell into the water, producing a new, two-tone burgundy silk tie.

As a result of all this, I walked into the training room sweating like a marathon runner, with a soggy, two-tone burgundy tie. To make things even more interesting, guess what kind of training I was doing—stress management! Like my first experience at Mutual of Omaha, I had good material. I wanted to do a good job, but I used the wrong strategy of preparing at the last minute.

After this second disaster, I was really frustrated. My dream was to be a corporate trainer who would have tremendous impact—someone who could teach powerful skills and excite people to take constructive action. But while my intentions were good, my strategies were not.

So I looked around to see what other corporate trainers in my area were doing. While they were definitely better than I, they still didn't have the zip and impact I wanted. Then one day I discovered Anthony Robbins through his books and audiotapes. I liked what I read and heard, so I went to see him in person. I was blown away by the experience! He was by far the best teacher I had ever seen. The strategies he used from the front of the room to get his points across were unbelievable in their impact. He educated, entertained, *and* inspired his audience!

I said to myself, "This guy is really on to something. I've got to learn the training strategies he's using!" So I went to work for Robbins Research International, Inc. As part of my first job with the company, I watched Tony present his one-day business seminar over fifty times. I also got to speak with him personally on numerous occasions. I took comprehensive notes on his presentation strategies, crystallized them into what I considered the ten most important keys, and started using the same strategies in my own training programs. The result was a dramatic improvement in my skills. Now I enjoyably travel around the world and speak to people who pay me very well to be there—because both my intentions and strategies are excellent!

In the last chapter you learned that empowering beliefs create *confidence* and that taking the appropriate action produces *competence*. You need both to be a Change Master.

In this chapter you will learn about strategies. When you use the right strategy, you know 1) what you're doing and 2) how to do it. Let's say you have a goal of seeing the moon. You've been to a lunar motivational seminar so you're excited. You believe you can see the moon. You have pictures of the moon on your walls at home. Each morning you repeat to yourself, "I will see the moon! I will see the moon! I will see the moon!" But if your strategy for seeing the moon is to look down at the floor, will you see it? No—because you're using the wrong strategy.

So you say to yourself, "This isn't working. I'd better go out and buy a telescope so I can look down with more power!" Well, I've got news for you—you'll never see the moon until you use the right strategy. Do you know what we call people with lots of enthusiasm but no idea of what they're doing? Loose cannons! To thrive on change, you need both a *positive belief* and an *effective strategy*. You need to be both confident (believe in what you're doing) and competent (know what you're doing).

Mental Strategies

There are two kinds of strategies: *mental* strategies and *physical* strategies. A mental strategy is *a set of steps you go through in your mind to achieve a particular result.* All great athletes know the power of mental strategies. They practice in their heads first before they play the game. They know practice makes perfect, so they practice perfectly in their minds before they take action.

Walt Disney had a creation strategy that brought pictures, sounds, and feelings to life. Where? First of all, in his mind. Then he made his mental creations a reality, both on the screen and in his theme parks.

Great spellers have a specific (and effective) mental strategy. First, in their mind's eye they *see* the word they want to spell, then they get a *feeling* that lets them know the spelling is correct. This visual spelling strategy is why misspelled words jump off the page and make great spellers wince. Conversely, what strategy do many poor spellers use? They *sound* out the word inside their head—an auditory mental spelling strategy. What are your chances of being right in the English language by "sounding it out"? Only about 20%!

Physical Strategies

The second kind of strategy, a physical strategy, is *a concrete set of actions you take to achieve an outcome.* You have a physical strategy you use each morning at home to get ready for the day. Top salespeople have a physical strategy, a specific set of actions they use over and over again to influence their customers to buy.

Every outcome has an optimal mental and physical strategy to achieve it. One of the real joys of life is discovering the strategies that work best to achieve the outcomes you desire. This book is full of the best strategies you can use to respond to, anticipate, create, and manage change in your life.

So, how can you not only optimize the strategies you are currently using but also create effective new strategies to meet the changing world ahead? There are four methods for improving your strategies.

FOUR STRATEGY-IMPROVEMENT MODELS

1. **MODELING**—Discovering the strategies others use to successfully create any outcome and duplicating their processes to obtain the same results

2. **"PLUSSING"**(a term coined by Walt Disney)— Improving your strategies a little bit at a time

3. **INNOVATION**—Improving your strategies massively

4. **REINVENTION**—Dropping virtually all your old strategies and adopting a new, improved set

IMPROVEMENT STRATEGY #1:

Modeling

Life is too short to make every possible mistake yourself. The quickest way to learn the strategies you need to thrive in our rapidly changing world is to *model successful people*. With modeling, you

1. Identify an outcome you want to create.

2. Find people who have already created the same outcome in their lives.

3. "Pick their brains" to discover the specific strategies they used to achieve their outcome.

4. Put those strategies to use in your life.

You can compress years of other people's experiences into hours by modeling their successes.

If possible, it's great to meet face to face with the people you wish to model. I call this strategy, "Take a rich person to lunch." If you can't meet with them, there are other ways to discover their strategies for success. You can attend their programs; read books, magazine or newspaper articles written by and about them; listen to their audiotapes; or talk with someone who knows them well. One of the best forms of modeling is to go to work for your model. This is what I did with Anthony Robbins.

Many corporations use modeling within their organization, duplicating the best practices of their most successful teams and individuals and then applying them across the board. Franchising is another very effective form of modeling. In the past year, I have worked with two extremely successful restaurant franchise operations— Golden Corral and Applebee's. I was amazed to see the precision with which they use the principle of modeling to spread effective strategies to hundreds of restaurants and thousands of employees across the U.S.

As powerful as modeling is, it's important to remember that *it will only get you to the point your model was at the time you modeled them.*

It will enable you to "catch up," but it will not take you beyond the level of success your model achieved with these strategies. This is why you also need to use plussing, innovation, and reinvention.

IMPROVEMENT STRATEGY #2:

Plussing

Walt Disney defined plussing as improving your personal life or business a little bit every single day. Remember, the difference between excellence and mediocrity can be a very fine line. The difference between the number one money winner on the PGA men's golf tour and those in the middle of the pack is 1.5 strokes per round—about a 2% difference!

I strongly recommend the book *Walt Disney—An American Original* by Bob Thomas. In it, Thomas relates, "During his visits to Disneyland, Walt was always plussing—looking for ways to improve the appearance of Disneyland and provide more pleasure for the customers. He would study an area and tell his staff, 'Let's get a better show for the customers; what can we do to give this place interest?'"

Members of Walt's staff once questioned spending $350,000 on a Christmas parade at Disneyland when the holiday crowds would come with or without the parade. Walt rejected their arguments, declaring, "We can't be satisfied, even though we'll get the crowds at Christmas time. We've always got to give them a little more. It'll be worth the investment. If they ever stop coming, it'll cost ten times that much to get them back."

Dissatisfaction is the basis of progress.
When we become satisfied, we become obsolete.

J. WILLARD MARRIOTT

Toyota knows the power of plussing. In 1984, Toyota received 2,150,000 suggestions from its employees for improvements in the way the company makes cars and does business. Toyota implemented an astonishing 96% of them!

Coach John Wooden knows the power of plussing. Wooden is generally recognized as the greatest college basketball coach of all time. The success of his teams and the quality of the people he helped shape are legendary in the sports world. In his final twelve years at UCLA, he won ten national championships!

A friend of mine, Brian Biro, visited Coach Wooden in his home in 1991. During the visit, Wooden described a set of three-ring binders he had compiled over the span of his twenty-seven years at UCLA (1949–75). In these binders Coach Wooden had noted every statistic, every drill, and every key observation he had made during every single practice. Wooden constantly looked for at least one small thing he wanted each player to improve upon at each practice. He recorded these plusses in the binders. As the season progressed, the team and individual players consistently improved a little at each practice— day by day, week by week, month by month. When NCAA tournament time rolled around in March, Wooden's teams were usually the best, and always *at* their best!

Coach Wooden didn't have to depend upon having the most talented players on his team, because he could depend upon plussing to constantly make everyone better. You can't always depend on having the best resources at your disposal. But you can always use plussing to improve what you have.

Think about it. Is failure usually one cataclysmic event? Rarely—more often than not, failure is created by a few errors in judgment repeated every day. After a while, these errors compound to create failure. For example, when people reach the age of sixty-five in the U.S., many don't have enough money saved to live the way they want to. How can you be short of money at sixty-five? All it takes is a few errors in judgment repeated every day. Don't save enough in your twenties. Don't save enough in your thirties, forties, fifties, or early sixties. Then you'll wake up one morning when you're sixty-five and say, "Oh, darn! I wish I would have!"

It's the same with your weight. You don't wake up one morning to discover twenty pounds of fat have magically become attached to your body. You put on twenty pounds by overeating and undermoving one day at a time.

Conversely, success is often a product of plussing, practicing a few simple habits every day. Financial success is certainly created this way. If you save $100 a month beginning at the age of twenty and let it compound at 10% interest, you would have over a *million dollars* at age sixty-five!

Plussing is how you lose twenty pounds and keep it off, by burning more calories than you eat each day. It's how you build success in any area of your life. Learn and grow a little each day by reading, listening to educational or inspirational audiotapes, and by taking rich people to lunch. Then take action by making a few small changes each and every day.

IMPROVEMENT STRATEGY #3:

Innovation

Plussing is improvement by evolution. Innovation is improvement by *revolution!* Innovations are occurring daily in the world of computers. The Hewlett-Packard LaserJet printer was just such an innovation. It was conceived by a CEO who told employees he wanted a laser printer that could be created in half the time and sell for one-third the current price.

Another example of innovation is the fuel injector. It made the carburetor obsolete while dramatically increasing the fuel efficiency of automobiles. In addition to being a master of plussing, Coach Wooden was an innovator. He was the first to successfully use the full-court pressure defense in college basketball.

[Our goal:] Double machine performance
at every price point every year.

ANDY GROVE
CEO, INTEL

Innovation can be difficult at times, because it requires that you either break unwritten rules and/or change the written rules currently operating in your world. Rules are necessary to provide the boundaries within which you act, but they also can limit exploration of the areas outside the boundaries—and it's in the outside areas that innovations are found.

Sol Price broke the unwritten rules of retailing when he started his Price Club discount warehouses. At the time, the four universally accepted unwritten rules of the retail business were:

1. You must build your store in an easily seen and easily accessible area.

2. You must advertise heavily to get customers into your store.

3. You must keep your store open for long hours seven days a week.

4. You must build an attractive store.

Here's what Sol did:

1. He built his stores in locations that could best be described as, "You can't get there from here!"

2. He did no advertising and required people to pay a yearly fee to get in the door.

3. He restricted store hours and made them so confusing that I still don't have much of an idea what the hours are (and I shop at Price Club regularly).

4. He built stores whose decor is best described as "early warehouse."

Today, Sol Price is an extremely wealthy person because he wasn't afraid to break a few unwritten rules and explore the uncharted areas where innovations are found.

The best example of how unwritten rules can limit your thinking is the nine dots exercise. Even if you've done this before, play along with me for two minutes. This is be your chance to be Sol Price for a day!

Here are the rules of the game:

1. You must connect all nine dots on page 97 with four straight lines.

2. You cannot lift your pen or pencil from the page.

3. You may retrace your line, but the retrace counts as another line.

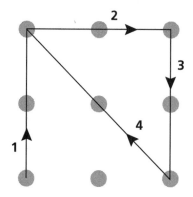

In the sample above, I drew four straight lines, but I missed one dot.

Now it's your turn. Copy the diagram from the next page into your journal or on a piece of paper, and connect all nine dots following the rules outlined above. If you're able to do it with four lines, do it with three lines using the same rules. I'll give you one hint for the three-line exercise: You may have to use your imagination and expand the page.

CONNECT THE NINE DOTS WITH FOUR LINES

How did you do? Now, take a look at the four-line solution below. The secret was to go *outside* the imaginary boundary formed by the nine dots. If you weren't able to connect the nine dots with four lines, why? Did you think you had to stay within the nine dots? If so, who established that rule? You did! Now, you might say, "In the sample you gave us, you stayed within the nine dots." That's true—and does that mean *you* had to? What chance do you have to innovate if you depend exclusively on how things were done in the past?

FOUR-LINE SOLUTION

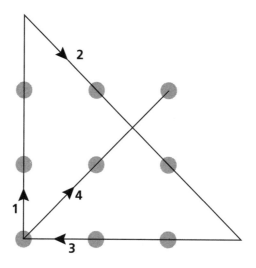

How about the three-line solution? If you couldn't come up with the answer, another unwritten rule probably was limiting your thinking—a rule that says, "All lines must go straight through the middle of the dots." Turn the page to see the three-line solution.

THREE-LINE SOLUTION

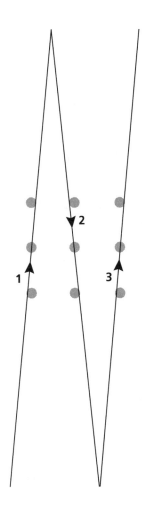

As you can see, line #1 can go through the left edge of the bottom dot, the middle of the center dot, and the right edge of the top dot. Then line #2 could turn, come back and go through the left edge of the top dot, the middle of the center dot, and the right edge of the bottom dot. The process repeats itself as line #3 comes up through the right line of dots.

I did this exercise a year ago with a group of engineers and one guy said, "Nate, you're the one who's blinded by your rules. You can connect all nine dots with one line, but you have to be a global thinker. Just run the line around the world!" He was right! We all have limiting rules. We all need to take off the blinders once in a while.

Another guy in the same group popped up and said, "I know another way to do it with one line. You've been using a pen that's too thin. Take a pen that makes a line two inches wide and it's a snap to connect the dots with one big fat line!" Someone else volunteered, "You could also fold the paper to bring all the dots together and connect them with one thin line."

Innovation breaks down rules. Remember, Orville Wright didn't have a pilot's license. He and his brother Wilbur were innovators—they thought outside the nine dots. They changed the rules of their day, and our world has never been the same since!

Innovative people ask innovative questions. Albert Einstein was definitely an innovator. He created the theory of relativity, part of which states, "At the speed of light, time stops." You might think Einstein locked himself in his office and did thousands of calculations to come up with such a breakthrough theory. Nope—here's how he did it. He was sitting at his kitchen table during lunch hour. He looked up at the clock on the wall and noticed it was exactly twelve o'clock. Then he asked himself a rather unusual question: "What if I could hop on a lightwave that came off this clock at exactly noon? No matter how far I might ride that lightwave off into the distance at the speed of light, would the lightwaves that came off the clock at the same time I did always say twelve noon?" In other words, if he traveled at the speed of light, would time stop?

Then he took it one step further and asked himself, "What if I could move *faster* than the speed of light and jump ahead of my lightwave to the lightwaves in front of me—the ones that came off the clock a split second *before* noon. If I did that, would time go *backward?*"

Have you ever sat at your kitchen table at noon? Probably. Have you ever looked up at the clock at noon? Probably. But have you ever asked yourself the question, "What if I could hop on a lightwave that came off this clock at exactly twelve noon?" Obviously not, or you could have come up with the same innovative answer Einstein did! Einstein got different answers because he asked different questions. Innovative people ask innovative questions.

As you may have noticed, using the words *what if* is a great way to start innovative questioning. *What if* automatically directs you to think outside the nine dots.

To be an innovator in your personal life, ask the following three questions on a regular basis. Be sure the words you write in the blanks create questions that get you thinking outside the nine dots.

1. **What if I could _____?**

   Example: "What if I could use my computer at home to make an extra $1000 a month?"

2. **What if I didn't have to _____?**

   Example: "What if I didn't have to go to the office five days a week?"

3. **What if I could _____ and _____?**

   (Come up with two things you didn't previously think you could do at the same time.)

   Example: "What if I could go back to school and maintain our current standard of living?"

To be an innovator in your business, ask these six questions:

1. **What if our company could _____?**

   Example: "What if our company could use laser technology to leapfrog over our competition?"

2. **What if our company didn't have to _____?**

   Example: "What if our company didn't have to do any of the manufacturing of our products?" (This is a question Nike asked from the very beginning!)

3. **What if our company could _____ and _____?**

   Example: "What if our company could lower prices and increase quality?" (This is a basic question that total-quality expert Dr. W. Edwards Deming, an American, got the Japanese to ask after World War II.)

4. **What if our customers could _____?**

   Example: "What if our customers could get our products without ever leaving their homes?" (Omaha Steaks built a huge mail order business by asking this question.)

5. **What if our customers didn't have to _____?**

   Example: "What if our customers didn't have to ever see a salesperson?" (Discount stockbrokers at Charles Schwab & Co. have used this idea to revolutionize the financial services industry.)

6. **What if our customers could _____ and _____?**

   Example: "What if our customers could order custom jeans and get them in two days?" (This is the question the Levi Strauss company has answered so successfully.)

If the answers to these innovative questions seem crazy, you're probably on the right track. The founder of Federal Express, Fred Smith, wrote a college term paper on the concept of overnight delivery. His paper received a C-minus! I would guess that the millions of dollars Federal Express has made off Fred Smith's innovative idea has eased the pain of his C-minus paper.

It's also important to remember that not all (or even most) innovative ideas work out. Innovative people accept this and embrace "failure"; innovative companies realize this and encourage lots of well-intentioned "failure."

Failure is our most important product.

R. W. JOHNSON

FORMER CEO, JOHNSON & JOHNSON

Using The Innovation–Plussing Combination

Many people mistakenly believe they can succeed long-term by having a few spurts of innovation while maintaining excellence between spurts. This idea is shown in Graph 1.

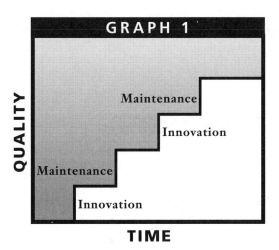

In reality, things never stay at the same level—they're either getting better or worse. If you don't focus on constantly making things better with plussing, guess which way they go?

Graph 2 depicts this cycle of intermittent innovation with a gradual decline between the innovations.

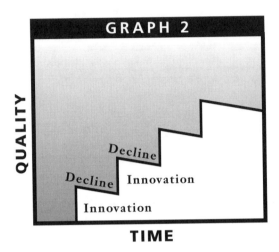

But when you combine innovation with plussing, you're on the fast track to success! Notice how the slope of the line in Graph 3 is much steeper than in Graphs 1 and 2.

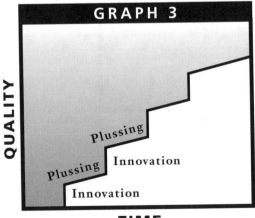

The chump-to-champ-to-chump cycle used to be three generations. Now it's about five years.

BILL MCGOWEN

FORMER CEO, MCI

IMPROVEMENT STRATEGY #4:

Reinvention

In many situations, especially in rapidly changing industries, modeling, plussing, and innovation aren't enough. In times of rapid change, you may occasionally need to reinvent as well. Reinvention is the dismantling and rebuilding of your business or your personal strategies. Because of fuel injectors, for example, carburetor manufacturers and skilled carburetor technicians had to reinvent both their businesses and their careers. In the last five years, tens of thousands of workers have had to reinvent their careers after their old skills were replaced by new technologies. Reinvention is absolutely critical in a world where at least 50% of the jobs that will be available in ten years haven't even been invented yet!

You hear a lot about business re-engineering these days. Re-engineering is another word for reinvention. In their landmark book *Re-engineering the Corporation*, Michael Hammer and James Champy define re-engineering as "the fundamental rethinking and radical redesign of business processes to achieve dramatic improvements in critical, contemporary measures of performance such as cost, quality, service, and speed." To survive in today's competitive and quickly changing world, many businesses must periodically re-engineer to survive. Likewise, many people may have to reinvent their business skills to thrive in our rapidly changing world.

Back in Chapter 2, you learned that IBM Credit Corporation can now process a new credit application in four hours instead of six days, with 5% fewer claims processors handling one hundred times the number of applications. This dramatic result was accomplished with re-engineering.

IBM started by asking one fundamental question: "How can we dramatically improve our credit issuance process?" They noticed the actual processing of a credit application only took ninety minutes. The rest of the time was consumed by sending the form from one department to another. So IBM decided to replace four specialists with one generalist. The generalist was then given comprehensive training and the latest technology to do the entire job.

Think about your own life and business. Are there any areas of your life where you need to ask, "How can I dramatically improve _____?"

When To Use Modeling, Plussing, Innovation, and Reinvention

You now have four strategies for improvement—modeling, plussing, innovation, and reinvention. When should you use each strategy in your business and personal life? Remember, if you use modeling exclusively, it will only catch you up to the other guy. Plussing is too slow in most situations, and it can discourage innovative thinking. In addition, the "other guy" may use innovation to leapfrog right past you! But innovation can't be created all the time and may take too long to implement. And you can't spend all your efforts reinventing yourself, continually dismantling and rebuilding.

I would recommend the following formulas.

In Your Personal Life

1. *Model* people you truly admire.

2. Improve your skills with *plussing* every day.

3. Transform your skills with *innovation* on a regular basis.

4. Be prepared to *reinvent* your life at a moment's notice.

In Your Business, If Your Products/Services Are at the Top of Your Industry

1. *Model* the parts of your competitors' products/services that are better than yours. Also, model the best practices in your own organization.

2. Improve your products, services, and business processes with *plussing* every day.

3. Improve your products, services, and business processes with *innovation* on a regular basis. Have a separate "renegade" team of people who constantly use innovation to improve your products and services. The sole purpose of this renegade team is to make your current products and services obsolete. Computer companies are constantly doing this.

4. *Reinvent* your business when needed.

If Your Products/Services Are in the Middle of the Pack or Lower

1. Use *modeling* to catch up quickly by duplicating your competitors' excellence in products/services/processes.

2. After you have caught up, use *plussing* to stay ahead.

3. Improve your products, services, and business processes with *innovation* on a regular basis.

4. *Reinvent* when needed!

With all this discussion of changing strategies, it's important to remember: **Even in changing times, there is a set of principles and habits you *never* want to change!**

Be firm in your adherence to the universal principles and the habits they foster. With this foundation, you can then be flexible with your strategies.

Now it's time to apply the modeling, plussing, innovation, and reinvention improvement strategies to your life by completing the Exercises for Action on the following page.

EXERCISES FOR ACTION

1. What are three outcomes you're committed to achieving in your life? Write them in your journal.

2. For each of these outcomes, who would be an excellent *model(s)* to have? List the models for each outcome and the ways you can learn more about these people.

3. What *plussing* strategies can you use to achieve these three outcomes?

4. What *innovative* strategies can you use to achieve these three outcomes?

5. Is it time to *reinvent* parts of your business or personal life? If so, how are you going to do it?

6. What are a few errors in judgment you have been committing each day that keep you from achieving these outcomes?

7. What are a few simple disciplines you are joyfully committed to doing each day that will enable you to be and do more?

This was your introduction to strategies. In Chapters 8 through 14, you will learn specific strategies you can use to react to, anticipate, create, and lead change both personally and professionally. But first, read on to learn how you can enjoyably move through your rapidly changing world.

It's time to discover . . .

Your Pathways to Action!

CHAPTER 7

Your Pathways
to Action

Take a close look at the word *action*. It's composed of three smaller words—*act*, *I*, and *on*. When you rearrange these three words, you will discover the true essence of the word action—"I act on." **I act on my principles and beliefs to create my destiny.** Action is the link between your resolutions and the realities they spark. After the mental creation of your desired outcome, action is the next step to the physical creation of your dreams.

Do you remember a time when action was effortless and you were on a roll? What did it feel like? What did you do? What kind of results did you get? Where would you end up if you could be on a roll consistently from this day forward? That's exactly what you will learn in this chapter—how to create the emotion necessary to start and keep rolling toward your dreams. **The first step of action is to put yourself in an empowering emotional state.** The emotions that drive your behavior are what I call *driver states*. At any moment, your actions will be heavily influenced by your driver state at that time. Have you ever said something or done something, and afterward you thought to yourself, "I can't believe I did that"? Why do you say or do negative things at certain times in your life? Because at that moment, you're in a negative driver state. When you're in negative states, you do negative things.

Have you ever had a time when you couldn't remember your own telephone number or how to spell a simple word? How can something like that happen? You really do know the number or the spelling, but the answer won't come because you're in a confused state. When you're in confused driver states, you do confused things.

The same is true with positive states. Let's say you've just been to a romantic movie with your partner. The movie director has manipulated the sights and sounds to put you in a romantic state. What do you do when you're in a romantic state? If you're lucky, you go home and have a romantic evening with your partner!

Visually, it looks like this:

DRIVER STATE ➡ ACTION

Great athletes know they have to be "psyched up" before the big game or they won't play to their full potential. The best actors know if they aren't ready before they go onstage, their performance will suffer. Top salespeople know they must get themselves into an enthusiastic state to maximize their chances of making the sale. The most effective managers keep their team in resourceful states so the team will want to take resourceful action. The ability to manage your own and other people's states is a vital key to your personal and professional success in our changing world!

There are two pathways you can use to create your own (or anyone else's) peak driver state: physical and mental.

PHYSICAL PATHWAY ➘

                      DRIVER STATE ➡ ACTION

➚

MENTAL PATHWAY

The Physical Pathway

Your physical pathway includes 1) the condition (level of health) of your body, and 2) the way you use your body. Anthony Robbins uses a very powerful example to illustrate how physical pathways affect emotions. Say there is a depressed man in the room next door. If you had to describe him without actually seeing him, how would you guess he looks? Would he be standing or sitting? Would his head be up or down? Would his eyes be focused up or toward the floor? Would his posture be erect or slumped? Would there be a lot of tension in his face, or would it be slack and loose? Would his breathing be deep or shallow?

Whenever I ask this question, almost everyone guesses, "Sitting, down, down, slumped, slack and loose, and shallow." And they're right. Why does everyone answer the same way? Because we're all experts! We've "been there and done that" on numerous occasions. You have to use your body in a certain way to feel depressed. And it's not easy; it takes effort to feel that bad!

I don't sing because I'm happy.
I'm happy because I sing!

WILLIAM JAMES

Let's do an exercise Anthony Robbins often uses to demonstrate the power of the physical pathway. Read the instructions on the next page, then put this book down and do the exercise.

The Depression Exercise

1. Sit in a chair with a slumped body position.

2. Put your head and eyes down.

3. Put a slack, pitiful look on your face.

4. Breathe shallowly and quickly.

5. Now, with your body in that position, try to feel excited and energized about something that really turns you on. Don't change your body position!

What did you experience? If you're like most people, one of two things happened. Either you changed your body position (smiled) to get the feeling of excitement and energy, or you didn't change your body position and couldn't get those feelings no matter how hard you tried.

Now, try another experiment. Read the instructions below, then put this book down and do the exercise.

The Excitement Exercise

1. Stand tall and look at the ceiling.

2. Put a big, silly grin on your face and raise your eyebrows.

3. Breathe deeply and fully.

4. With your body in that position, try to get depressed or upset about something. If you're politically conservative, think of those "bleeding heart" liberals. If you're more liberal, think of those "heartless" conservatives. Come on, get depressed!

How did you do? You probably couldn't do it, because, as Anthony Robbins says, "Emotion is created by motion." As long as you hold your body in an excited position, you can't access the depressed feeling. The message is clear: Look up in life! After all, Michelangelo painted his heavenly masterpiece on the Sistine Chapel ceiling—he didn't paint it on the floor!

Movement sends messages to your brain and communicates your emotions to other people. Here's an example of sending positive messages to your own brain. Say it's three o'clock in the afternoon. You're at your desk, feeling tired. How do you change your feelings? Simple—get up and do something! Take a walk, stretch a little, change your position, take a few deep breaths. You'll feel much better as a result!

Jangle loosely when you walk.

SATCHEL PAIGE

Movement can also send messages to other people's brains. Have you ever been at a presentation where the speaker walks up to the stage v-e-r-y s-l-o-w-l-y with no energy in his body and a blank expression on his face? He steps behind the podium and pulls out a three hundred-page script. Then he begins speaking v-e-r-y, v-e-r-y s-l-o-w-l-y with no emotion in his voice. He says, "My name is Dr. Melvin Boringovich III, and for the next nine hours or so I'm going to be talking to you about . . ." What pops into your head? "This is going to be a loooooooooong day!" His movements have sent a clear message to your brain.

An Easterner who walked into a Western saloon one day was amazed to see a dog sitting at a table playing poker with three men. "Can that dog really read the cards and play poker?" he asked. "Yeah, but he ain't much of a card player," replied one of the men. Whenever he gets a good hand, he wags his tail."

ANONYMOUS

Another great example of movement sending messages occurred in the 1960 presidential debate between Richard Nixon and John F. Kennedy. The debate was broadcast both on radio and, for the first time, on television. The majority of people who listened to the radio thought Nixon won the debate. But the majority of people who watched the debate on TV thought Kennedy won. Why? Kennedy was much better at sending "elect me" visual (physical pathway) messages than Nixon.

> *Every man carries in his eye*
> *the exact indication of his rank.*
>
> RALPH WALDO EMERSON

Your physical pathway is the fastest and best way to mange your own or anyone else's driver states. Your mom knew this. Remember when you were a kid and you told her you were bored? What did she say? "Why don't you go outside and do something?" She was right!

Your mom also knew the second way to manage driver states—she knew how to harness the power of your mental pathway.

The Mental Pathway

Three years ago, I was sitting on the rooftop of my friend Chip Eichelberger's home, perched on a hillside in Cardiff, California about a half a mile from the Pacific Ocean. Chip said, "I've got a quiz for you. Look west and tell me what you see." I said, "I see a beautiful blue ocean with an orange-red sun just about ready to set." He replied, "That's what I see, too. That's why we bought this place. But you would be amazed at the number of people who look off my rooftop and see those telephone poles and wires about a hundred yards down the hill. They say it ruins the view." I hadn't even noticed the poles and wires until he mentioned them.

When you look at the world, do you focus on the poles and wires or the oceans and sunsets? They're both there. When you focus on the poles and wires, you're using your mental pathway to create a negative driver state. This will influence you to take negative actions which produce negative results. The whole chain of events started with your "pole and wire" mental focus.

Conversely, when you focus on the ocean and the sunset, you're using your mental pathway to create a positive driver state. This will influence you to take positive actions which produce positive results. This chain of events was started with your "ocean and sunset" metal focus.

Watch your mental focus; it directs your thoughts.

Watch your thoughts; they lead to emotions.

Watch your emotions; they spark actions.

Watch your actions; they become habits.

Watch your habits; they build character.

Watch your character; it determines your direction.

Watch your direction; it creates your destiny.

ADAPTED FROM QUOTE FROM SAMUEL SMILES

As you can see, the mental pathway is the second way you can manage your driver states. There are thousands of things you could focus on mentally at any moment in time. How many can your brain handle at once? One thing at a time. Make sure that the one thing you focus on during your day enjoyably gets you where you want to go.

Here's an example of selective mental focus. In your journal or on a blank piece of paper, draw an exact picture of the face of your watch without looking at it.

Now look at the face of your watch very closely. How accurately did your drawing match the real thing? If you're like most people, not very well. You glance at your watch dozens of times a day, but you're focusing on the time, not the face. That's why the watch face didn't register precisely in your brain.

The real act of discovery consists not in finding

new lands, but seeing with new eyes.

MARCEL PROUST

Here are three other examples of mental focus in action.

1. **"Don't look at me like that!"**

My wife and I were at an Embassy Suites hotel in Palm Springs, California about three years ago. We went down to have the complimentary breakfast that Embassy Suites always serves. There were probably two dozen people in the line waiting to place their order, and three times that number already eating. The amazing thing was that there were only two cooks preparing everything—the eggs, the omelets, the toast, the pancakes, the hash browns, the bacon, the sausage! It was a pleasure to see these two men in such resourceful driver states, performing quickly and effectively.

However, it didn't last long. Through a side door walked a man who was obviously the cooks' supervisor. He didn't say one word. He didn't have to—he just crossed his arms and watched the cooks closely, occasionally writing in a notebook. What do you think happened to the cooks' performance? It went down the tubes! Their mental focus changed completely. They stopped focusing on *what* they were doing and started focusing on *how* they were doing. That put them in a questioning, tentative, flustered driver state, and they started messing up orders all over the place.

Moral: As you do a task, focus on what *you're doing. After you're done, you can focus on* how *you did.*

2. The 95% or the 5%?

If your company is like most organizations, it's probably 95% good, great, and wonderful, and 5% not so good, great, and wonderful. That's the way organizations are. What happens to employees who perpetually focus on the lousy 5%? They're constantly talking to their friends about the 5%. They call each other after work and rehash the 5%. The lousy 5% is always on their minds. If their mental focus is on the negative, what kind of state will they be in on a regular basis? You guessed it—a negative state. What kind of actions does this lead to? Negative actions. What kind of results do the negative actions create? Negative results. After they experience the negative results, what do they say? "See, this place is screwed up, just like I told you!" It's not the place. It's their mental focus.

Moral: Spend most of your time focusing on the 95%.

3. A "Brain Burp"

Let's suppose you're walking down the street and a friend of yours named Frank comes up to you and stomps on your foot. As you're walking away upset, a brain surgeon approaches you and says, "I saw what Frank did to you. I just want you to know Frank was in my office last week and we discovered a 'brain burp'—a little pocket of air in his brain. Because of this condition, sometimes Frank acts without thinking. He can't help it. I just thought you should know."

Two minutes before you were ticked off. How are you feeling now? Probably sympathetic and understanding. Why? Because now you know that Frank has a brain burp—a physical reason why he acted the way he did. It wasn't the incident per se that made you mad. It was your mental focus that created the upset.

"So, what's the point?" you may be asking. The point is we all have our own little psychological brain burps— conditioned patterns of behaving stupidly, without thinking, in certain situations. We all have them, don't we? At one time or another, we've all said, "Boy, I wish I hadn't done that!" Or we've had moments where someone does something awful and we feel offended.

For me, the brain burp metaphor acts as a "pattern interrupt." It breaks my conditioned pattern of automatically getting upset when people do something I don't agree with. It changes my mental focus to why they did what they did. If there is a reason for their actions, even if I don't agree with it, at least I don't have to act upset. Instead, I can feel sympathy for these poor folks who just brain burped in public. You can arrange your mental focus to make yourself feel almost any emotion in any situation. Why not choose to feel good instead of bad?

What if next week your boss says or does something annoying? If you find yourself getting upset, let a little smile creep over your lips as you think, "Oh, she's got a brain burp! It's one of those boss brain burps!"

If you have teenage children, you know they have *multiple* brain burps! So, the next time your teenager says or does something that is totally off course and you find yourself getting upset, think about all those teenage brain burps you used to have. And realize that it's probably something your child will grow out of—sooner rather than later, you hope!

This brain burp concept is useful because it gives you the opportunity to react more resourcefully in stressful situations. And when you're in a more resourceful state, you will handle the situation better. Perhaps you can even take action to help these unfortunate souls cure their brain burps!

Life does not consist mainly—or even largely—
of facts and happenings. It consists mainly
of the storm of thoughts that is forever
blowing through one's head.

MARK TWAIN

If the mental pathway is so important, where should you put your mental focus to make the most of change? Here's the general rule: **For optimal results in your life and your business, focus on anything that is in alignment with universal principles and enjoyably gets you where you want to go in life—as long as the focus doesn't hurt anyone else in the process and preferably helps them.**

I recommend five Essential Mental Focus Areas that will help you keep yourself consistently in a resourceful driver state.

Five Essential Mental Focus Areas

1. Focus on outcomes first and processes second.

It's all too easy to get caught up in *doing* things and forget *why* you're doing them. It's important to keep focused on the result rather than the means.

A clearly defined outcome is the destination you want to achieve, and processes are the bricks that make up the path to the destination. When your destination is clear, it's relatively easy to lay the bricks in a pattern that creates a direct path. When your destination is not clear, you feel confused and don't know where to place your bricks. You end up laying bricks randomly so that you feel and look busy; or else you stop laying bricks at all because you don't see a payoff. Do you ever see this concept in action at your place of business?

Let me give you an example. When I do training programs for corporations and associations, they will often ask, "What are some of your program topics that would be appropriate for our group?" That is certainly a fair question, but it's putting the cart before the horse. What I really need to know first are the outcomes a company or group wants from my presentation. Only then can I put together the exact program that will give them the outcomes they desire.

Recently I spoke with a man named Eddie, who was sitting next to me on an airplane. He worked for a railroad, and he told me a great story about the dangers of putting processes before outcomes. From the very beginning, all railroad companies refueled and serviced their locomotives by first disconnecting them from the rest of the train, then having a separate yard crew drive them to a service center on the outer boundary of the railroad yard. There the crew would pick up a different set of locomotives, drive them back to the rest of the train, and reconnect them. In addition, the air brakes on each car had to be inspected whenever a locomotive was disconnected from the rest of the train. This whole process would take about eight hours. How's that for a long, complicated, and expensive process?

One day about five years ago, someone finally questioned the process; he was thinking outside the nine dots. This person suggested, "Let's refuel and service the locomotives with mobile fuel and service trucks. We'll never have to unhook the locomotives. We can service them right there on the same track, and we can eliminate the constant air brake inspections because all the cars will stay hooked together." After overcoming the ardent objections of those who managed and carried out the old process (big surprise, right?), that's exactly what the railroad did. Now Eddie's company can service and refuel a locomotive in one hour, with 40% fewer people and 50% fewer locomotives than were required previously!

It's crucial that you have specific and measurable outcomes in your life and your business. It's equally critical that you know exactly where you are right now. Then you can create the processes to get you from where you are now to where you want to go. As you do this, be on the lookout for phrases like, "We've never done it that way before," or "This is how we do it around here." That's a sure sign that processes are coming before outcomes!

2. Selectively focus on the past, present, or future as needed.

People who thrive on change are time travelers who use the past, present, and future to their advantage. Like Ebenezer Scrooge in Dickens' *A Christmas Carol*, they pop in and out of the past, present, and future to gain the knowledge, insight, or inspiration they need.

THE PRESENT

Successful time travelers spend most of their time in the present. Like the cooks at the Embassy Suites, they know their performance will be optimized when their focus is on the here and now. They follow the rule, "Wherever you're at, be there!" They are there with their families, kids, friends, hobbies, and jobs.

THE PAST

There are two ways successful time travelers use the past to gain the wisdom they need to guide themselves in the present. First, they learn from the past. They learn from both "positive" and "negative" experiences. Remember, you never know whether the experience is truly negative or positive at the end of the day. Many of those "negative" experiences end up shaping your life positively in the long run. And you can always choose to create a positive meaning from almost any experience.

Second, these time travelers access the past to remember the good times. When they focus on the good times, they can feel as great now as they did then. Try it yourself. Think of a time in your past when you had a great experience. Go through that experience in your mind from beginning to end. Relive it fully—see what you and the people around you (if any) were doing, hear what you and the others were saying, feel yourself doing the things you did. Now, notice how you feel in the present. If you feel great or even pretty good, if there's a smile on your face, congratulations—you've successfully used the past to feel good in the present!

Resourceful feelings are nice to experience in and of themselves, *and* they can help you take better actions in the present. When I work with athletes, I have them mentally go back to a time when they were performing at peak levels.

I get them to experience everything they saw, heard, and felt. Then, when they're in that peak driver state, I have them play their sport. It's amazing how dramatically their performance improves. Peak states lead to peak performance!

The opposite is also true. Have you seen a really bad TV show in the last year or two? If you answered yes, when the show came back in reruns during the summer, did you go back and watch it again, or videotape it so you could see it two or three more times? I doubt it, because you were smart enough to know it was a bad program. Now, have you had a "negative" experience in the past year or two? If you answered yes, do you ever go back and replay it again and again in your mind? Many people do. If you do that, you get to feel bad all over again, and this bad state will produce bad actions and bad results.

Do you know anyone who is "living" in a negative past— maybe someone you know very, very well? How effective is this person in the present? How much does he or she enjoy life? Wouldn't you love to drag this person out of the past and into the present? You can do this by consistently redirecting this person's mental focus. Say, "I know you may have had some painful experiences in the past. But it's your choice whether you allow them to hold you back, or decide to use them to become stronger. I have a question for you: What did you learn from that situation? And how are you going to use it to improve your life now?" Don't let this person (or yourself) wallow around in the hog slop of the past. Redirect your thinking to the present by asking questions that help access more positive driver states.

THE FUTURE

It's amazing that we humans have the capacity not only to get upset about what's happening today or has already happened, but also to get upset *in advance!* We don't have to wait for something bad to happen to us—we can feel bad about the future by focusing on something bad that *might* happen! All anxiety and fear are nothing more than an inappropriate use of our ability to imagine the future.

My life has been filled with terrible misfortunes—
most of which never happened.

MARK TWAIN

How do the best time travelers use the future? They create the future of their dreams rather than their nightmares. Like President Kennedy and his dream of putting a man on the moon, they focus on their dreams and goals, which puts them in the driver states that will produce the behaviors that will lead to the fulfillment of their dreams. It's the belief cycle in action!

The best time travelers also use the future to anticipate and proactively make any changes necessary to achieve their dreams. Using a surfing metaphor, they anticipate the wave so they can start paddling in advance to be able to ride it. If they didn't anticipate the wave, it might turn them head over heels. When they anticipate the wave, they can have the thrill of riding the wave to shore.

The past, the present, or the future—the choice is yours!

3. Focus on limitations and problems 2% of the time, and on resources and solutions 98% of the time.

People who thrive on change aren't Pollyannas. They aren't 100% positive thinkers. Every once in a while they look at their gardens to see if there are any weeds. If there are, they quickly pull out the weeds and get on with it. If they didn't do this occasionally, the weeds would take over their gardens.

Every once in a while, you need to sit down, examine your life, and take a good look at any limitations and problems. Then you can focus your resources on the solutions that are going to make things better. It's best to analyze your problems in ways that transform problems into challenges, by using a "solutions/resources" focus. Don't waste your time bemoaning your limitations or figuring out why this terrible problem is in your life. Those strategies will get you nowhere. Instead, ask yourself, "How can I solve this challenge?" and "What *resources* do I already have—or need—to handle this challenge now?" This will give you the action orientation you need to solve the challenge.

The actor Christopher Reeve would have every right to focus on limitations and problems. As you'll recall, in 1995 he was thrown from his horse while jumping in a competition. He landed on his head and broke his neck. He is now a quadriplegic and needs a respirator to breathe. Less than a year after his accident he was interviewed by Larry King on CNN. Larry asked him if he'd ever gotten depressed as a result of his condition. Christopher replied, "No, because I always focus on what I have, not what I don't have. I have my life, my family, my friends. And I've discovered I have tens of thousands of friends I didn't even know about. I have much more than I lost." Think about this inspiring example the next time you find yourself focusing on your own "problems" more than 2% of the time!

Ross Perot knows the power of focusing on resources and solutions. He founded Electronic Data Systems (EDS) in 1962 and built it into a billion dollar company. In 1986, General Motors bought EDS for a total of $2.55 billion in cash and stock. Perot's personal share of the sale was worth $700 million. As part of the deal, Perot was put on the board of directors at GM, but, as you'll recall, he didn't last long. The lack of action-oriented solution finding at GM drove him nuts. Perot said, "When someone sees a snake at EDS, we kill it! When someone sees a snake at GM, the first thing they do is form a committee on snakes. Then they bring in an outside consultant on snakes. They write a strategic plan for getting rid of snakes. Then six layers of managers delegate someone to kill the snake." Ross knows that if you don't kill the snake when it's small, you might be dealing with a monster later.

Be sure to focus on limitations and problems 2% of the time, and on resources and solutions 98% of the time.

4. **Focus on learning and growing.**

A continual focus on learning and growing is absolutely necessary to thrive in changing times. When things change, you must change! Remember Aunt Millie? She knew how to learn and grow. That's why people like her are so highly prized in the business world today. They're flexible and adaptable enough to change with the changing times.

Tony Bennett has been singing professionally for over forty years, yet he is still learning and growing. Recently an interviewer asked Bennett why his popularity was soaring, especially with younger audiences. He replied, "I'm finally learning how to sing now. I just learned a new vocal technique from watching [Luciano] Pavarotti. It's made me a much better singer!" If a master who has been at it for over forty years can still be learning and growing, so can you.

They know enough who know how to learn.

HENRY ADAMS

CEO, MOTOROLA, INC.

Motorola is consistently on *Forbes Magazine*'s list of the best-run corporations in America. Motorola knows the value of helping its employees learn. Motorola calculates it earns $33 for every $1 spent on training. Do you put the same value on your personal training program?

Our employees look at change and learning as job security.

HARRY QUADRACCI

CEO, QUAD/GRAPHICS

5. Focus on providing value.

When you respect others, they will tend to respect you in return. When you treat others well, they will tend to treat you well in return. When you provide value to other people, they will tend to give value back to you.

Back in the '60s, when I was in college, the first rule of business was, "Find a need and fill it." It was a simple rule for simple times. "Find a need and fill it" doesn't work quite so well in today's world. Things are changing too rapidly, the competition is too intense, and the customers' expectations are too high. When I use the word *customer*, I mean all the customers in your personal life—your teammates at work, your family, your friends—as well as your business customers.

To succeed today, you need to follow the new first rule of business. This rule takes two forms, depending on whether you want a problem focus (Part One) or a product/service focus (Part Two).

The new First Rule of Business, Part One, is, **"Actively discover your customers' problems, and then uniquely and quickly over-solve them."** Dell Computer is the perfect example of this approach. It actively discovers its customers' problems thousands of times each day by talking to people as their orders are taken on the phone. Then it uniquely (configuring each computer to the customer's exact specifications) and quickly (assembling the customer's computer the next day) over-solves the problem. Is it any wonder that Dell is a leader in the industry, even though it has far fewer resources than "the big boys"?

The new First Rule of Business, Part Two, takes a product/ service focus. It is, **"Create a desire for your product or service, then uniquely and quickly exceed it with value."** With this focus, you direct your attention to creating a desire for products and services that people don't even know they need yet. After all, customers didn't ask Thomas Edison to invent a light bulb, or Spencer Fry to create Post-it® Notes, or Akio Morita to develop the Walkman®, or Steven Jobs and Steve Wozniak to build the first personal computer. But imagine doing without these products or services now!

Let's examine the four elements of the new First Rule of Business, Part Two.

1. *Create a desire for your product or service . . .*

When I ask business audiences around the country, "How many of you have used a Post-it Note in the past week?" 90% of them raise their hands. How would you like to be 3M, with a 90% market penetration and one billion dollars in sales each year on just one product? What's truly amazing is when 3M introduced Post-it Notes, an extensive marketing and sales campaign in four test cities revealed the product was a loser. Nobody in the office supply business wanted to sell an unknown product that had a comparatively high price (compared to staples and paper clips) and a low profit margin.

But there were two men at 3M who really had their jobs on the line with this product. They loved Post-its and couldn't see why everyone else didn't love them, too. So they went to Richmond, Virginia (one of the test market cities) to see what was wrong. In a last-ditch effort to save the product from the scrap heap, they took a couple of boxes of Post-it Notes and went up and down the business district of Richmond, giving the product away. Now, as you probably know, once you use Post-its, you're hooked! Richmond was hooked, too. Reorders came in at a 90% rate, double that of any other successful office product. Today, Post-it Notes are a billion-dollar-a-year winner for 3M.

The moral of this story is simple: *One way to be successful in business is to create a desire for a product that people don't think they need, then uniquely and quickly exceed their expectations with value.* That's what Federal Express did in the mail delivery industry. The U.S. Postal Service, United Parcel Service, and Emery Worldwide all asked their customers, "Would you pay more for what what it's going to cost us to provide overnight delivery?" The answer was a resounding, "No! We won't pay that amount for overnight delivery." But Fred Smith didn't believe it. He knew this innovative concept would work and created Federal Express to prove it. I'm sure you've heard the story of Federal Express's early years—

the company barely survived in the beginning. It was held together by a group of people with a common dream who finally created a desire for overnight delivery. And it's a good thing for business that Federal Express stuck with it. Overnight delivery has extended project deadlines by at least two days for businesses across the nation and around the world. Dozens of other companies have jumped on the overnight service bandwagon, expanding the kinds of services offered and keeping rates relatively low.

Not only does your company have to provide tremendous value to survive in our rapidly changing times, you must constantly discover new ways of providing value for those closest to you, as well as your employer and your customers. In my travels around the world, I've met hundreds of people who have wonderful jobs because they created a demand for their services. They didn't wait for a job opening to be posted.

2.　*. . . then uniquely . . .*

Not only did Federal Express create a desire, it got the idea into the marketplace first. Federal Express is unique to this day. Have you noticed that it's maintaining its uniqueness by being one step ahead of the competition? Here are four more examples of the power of being unique.

- Remember Southwest Airlines? It's certainly unique, not only in the joy its employees bring to each flight but in the way it has organized flight scheduling to keep costs down. Southwest's fares are almost always the lowest in any marketplace where it flies.

- Back in 1976, there was a pitcher for the Detroit Tigers who attracted huge amounts of attention by being unique. His name was Mark "The Bird" Fidrych. He would stalk the pitcher's mound like a bird, and talk out loud to the ball before he threw it!

While Fidrych had excellent skills, it was his uniqueness that put him in the national spotlight.

- In 1990, the long distance telephone company MCI had a 13% market share. In 1993, the figure had risen to 20%, an increase of more than 50% in three years. One reason for MCI's success is that it continually comes out with unique services such as "Friends and Family," "1-800-COLLECT," and "1-800-MUSIC NOW."

- In the spring of 1995, the musical group Hootie & the Blowfish stormed to the top of the charts. It wasn't because their music was so unique—it was the group itself that stood out. They were so normal in a world of "weird" musical groups!

You, too, need to be unique in today's marketplace. You need to have the principles, habits, beliefs, and strategies that make you stand out and influence people to want to employ you, work with you, or buy your products or services.

3. *. . . and quickly . . .*

Dealing with rapid, constant, and worldwide change is like dancing with an elephant—you're either quick or you're dead! Because of intense competition, it's critical that you provide value quickly. That's what MCI did with its "1-800-COLLECT" service. The time period from idea to program launch was a mere eleven weeks! Here are a few examples.

- Sony knows the value of quickness. It invented the first Walkman in 1979, and from 1979 to 1993, it created 227 different models. That's an average of one new model every thirty-four days! How would you like to be one of Sony's competitors and try to keep up with that pace?

- Motorola used to take a month to complete orders for customized pagers. Now it sends orders by computer to its manufacturing plant in Florida, which builds, tests, and prepares the pager for shipment in less than two hours!

- The Rubbermaid Corporation thrives in the extremely competitive consumer products industry because it is quick with product development. It creates more than one new product every day!

You need to be quick, too. You must have a sense of urgency about learning, growing, and providing value for all the customers in your life.

4. *. . . exceed their expectations with value.*

With the old First Rule of Business, you found a need and filled it. Filling it isn't enough in today's highly competitive marketplace. As a company, you must exceed your customers' needs with value—by providing extremely high-quality products and services. Quality is the single greatest key to long-term profitability. In 1990, companies that provided low-quality products and services had a 1% return on sales and lost market share at the rate of 2% a year. Companies that provided high-quality products and services had a 12% return on sales and gained market share at a rate of 6% a year!

Walt Disney constantly focused on providing value. In his early years, he was paid $5,000 each for some of his cartoon short subjects, which had cost $7,000 each to make. When someone questioned his logic, Walt replied, "They'll pay more the next time if these are great!"

Walt continued this practice of providing high quality at his theme parks. When he was walking around Disneyland as it was being built, if something pleased him he would say, "I think they'll go for this," or "They're going to eat this up." If he saw something he didn't like, he would say, "That's not good enough for them," or "They'll expect something better!" By focusing on constantly providing value, Walt achieved his dream of using imagination to bring happiness to millions.

You must do the same in your professional life. You need to give your company more value than you're paid for. If your employer or customers/clients pay you $20 an hour for your services, give them at least $21 an hour in value. That way you will drastically increase your chances of being promoted (your employer) or receiving additional business (your customers/clients).

You also need to give the people you care about more love and respect than they expect, so that their love and respect are returned to you and given to others. You need to enthusiastically and lovingly jump into the pond of life each day and create ripples (or waves) that positively affect the whole pond.

We've covered a lot of important material in this chapter. It's vital that you grasp the power of controlling your own physical and mental pathways so that you can feel and act in ways that produce the results you desire. If you don't control these pathways, external events will, and the emotions, actions, and results created will not be the ones you desire. When you do control your mental and physical pathways, the emotions, actions, and results you create will move you closer to the life you desire. You will move from *reacting* to life to *choosing* the life of your dreams.

Don't stop now! The most important part of the chapter begins on the next page.

EXERCISES FOR ACTION

1. Think of a specific time when you were in a
   resourceful driver state, a time when you were on
   a roll and achieving fantastic results in your life.
   Describe your physical and mental pathways at
   that time by answering the following questions.

   A. What did you do *physically* when you were in this
      resourceful driver state? How did you use your body?
      How did you stand? How did you breathe? How did
      you move? What was your energy like—smooth and
      focused, or sharp and explosive, for example? Write a
      short description in your journal.

   B. What did you do *mentally* when you were in this
      resourceful driver state? What were you thinking about?
      What pictures were in your mind? How were you feeling?
      Did you say something to yourself, like, "You can do
      it!" or "Go get 'em"? What did you have to believe in
      order to be in this resourceful state? Can you remember
      the syntax—the specific sequence of thoughts and
      emotions—you experienced when you were in this
      driver state? Make a few notes now.

2. Now, think of a specific time when you were in an unresourceful driver state. (This is an especially good exercise if
   you find yourself in this particular state on any kind of a
   regular basis.) Describe this unresourceful state using the
   same process as #1. What were the physical and mental
   pathways you used to get into this unresourceful state?

3. It's easy to change an unresourceful driver state to a more resourceful one. The next time you find yourself getting into that unresourceful state, try adding some elements of the physical and mental pathways of your *resourceful* state. For example, if you stand with your head up, chest out, feet planted, and fists clenched when you're resourceful, change your physiology to adopt those characteristics. If the words you say to yourself when you're in that resourceful state are, "You can do it!" say those same words to yourself in the same tonality. Then notice the difference in your state!

4. Think of a specific time when it would be valuable to be in an enthusiastic driver state. What physical and mental pathways would work the best for you to create that state? Describe both pathways in your journal.

5. Review each of the Five Essential Mental Focus Areas. How are you currently using them in your life? In which areas have you been especially effective in using these five tools (even though you weren't necessarily aware of them before)? In which areas do you need some improvement?

    A. **Focus on outcomes first and processes second.**

    B. **Selectively focus on the past, present, or future as needed.**

    C. **Focus on limitations and problems 2% of the time, and on resources and solutions 98% of the time.**

    D. **Focus on learning and growing.**

    E. **Focus on providing value.**

In this chapter, you've learned how to harness the awesome power of your physical and mental pathways. In the next chapter, you will learn one of the most effective ways to direct your mental pathway.

Read on to discover why . . .

Questions Are the Keys!

CHAPTER 8

Questions Are the Keys

Put this book down for thirty seconds and answer this question: "What are you proudest of in your life right now?" Come up with at least two emotional answers.

Why are you feeling the emotion of pride right now? Because you asked yourself the right *question*. Questions are the easiest and best way to direct your own or anyone else's mental focus.

Why are questions so effective? To understand this, it helps to use a metaphor about the way your brain stores information. Picture your brain as a filing cabinet full of files. In each file is a memory or a group of related memories. These memories often have an emotion attached to them. Questions are one of the most effective tools to open the files in your brain. Once a file is opened, the information (and the emotion attached to it) in that file is available for your use.

For each file in your brain, there is a specific question that will open it. You just need to discover what that question is. Ask and you shall receive!

I believe that questions work even better than affirmations in directing mental focus and initiating action. With affirmations, you repeat a statement to yourself. You get up in the morning and say, "I'm motivated! I'm motivated! I'm motivated!" However, if you're not feeling great, your brain says, "No way I'm motivated!" and you're worse off than you were before.

A much more effective approach for getting your day off to a great start is to ask yourself the following Morning Questions every day. The Morning Questions were created by Anthony Robbins and appear in his best-selling book, *Awaken the Giant Within*.

Read each question and then answer it with emotion. Come up with at least two answers for each one!

THE MORNING QUESTIONS

1. What am I happiest about in my life now?
2. What am I most excited about in my life now?
3. What am I most proud of in my life now?
4. What am I most grateful for in my life now?
5. What am I enjoying most in my life now?
6. What am I most committed to in my life now?
7. Who do I love? Who loves me?

I strongly urge you to make a copy of the Morning Questions and tape it to a mirror you use each day, or attach it to the visor of your car and answer the questions on the way to work. Do the Morning Questions for one week and you'll do them for the rest of your life!

Another key time to ask yourself questions is when you're upset about a "negative" change in your life. You can "un-upset" yourself by answering the following Realignment Questions which I created.

THE REALIGNMENT QUESTIONS

1. Concerning this situation, what possible information am I not currently aware of that would change how I feel about it?

2. In addition to the meaning I'm currently attaching to the situation, what *else* could this mean?

3. What could be the other person's "brain burp"?

4. How unimportant will this be in five years?

5. How can I change my physical and mental pathways *right now* to create a more resourceful driver state?

6. In this resourceful driver state, what action could I take *right now* to clear up the misunderstanding?

Let's use the Realignment Questions in a hypothetical situation. Someone tells you a friend of yours said something extremely negative about you. You find yourself getting upset; then you ask yourself the following.

1. **Concerning this situation, what possible information I'm not currently aware of would change how I feel about it?**

"After all, I really don't know exactly what my friend said. I'm getting it secondhand from another person. It's probably just a communication error. It's possible that my friend may have been in such a negative state that he said something he regrets now. I doubt it, but I know I've done that myself on occasion."

2. **In addition to the meaning I'm currently attaching to the situation, what *else* could this mean?**

   "It could just be a communication mix-up. It could mean that the other person thinks this is a way to get on my good side. It could mean that my friend is human and messed up in the moment."

3. **What could be the other person's "brain burp"?**

   "His brain burp could be that he thinks the only way to make himself look good is to make other people look bad. My friend's brain burp could be that he gets emotionally carried away sometimes and doesn't think about what he's saying."

4. **How unimportant will this be in five years?**

   "In five years, I won't even remember this incident. It's a drop in the bucket."

5. **How can I change my physical and mental pathways right now to create a resourceful driver state?**

   "I'm going to put myself in a resourceful physiology and focus on all the great times my friend and I have had together."

6. **In this resourceful state, what action can I take right now to clear up the misunderstanding?**

   "I'm going to give my friend a call to see what really happened."

The moral of this example is: *If you don't like the answers you're getting in life, learn to ask better questions!*

Questions are essential tools that direct how we use our brains. Outstanding people ask outstanding questions. Creative people ask creative questions. Unusual people ask unusual questions. Innovators like Albert Einstein ask innovative questions no one else is asking.

The challenge is that most people tend to ask themselves the same questions over and over each day. That's why they get the same answers throughout their lives. **To get different answers in your life, you must ask different questions.** This book is designed to help you do just that. What would happen if, in the days ahead, you asked questions you'd never asked before? Are you ready for the power and promise of the new answers you will create?

Have you ever had a conversation with a friend who's going on and on about a "bad" experience that just happened to her? You saw that she was in an unresourceful state, so you decided to help her by changing her mental focus. You asked her, "How are your kids doing?" or "What's happening at work?" or "Hey, I heard you had a great round of golf the other day. Can you tell me about it?" What usually happens? Your friend will start talking about her kids, or work, or golf, and forget about the bad experience. By shifting her focus to something pleasurable she cares about, you helped her change her state.

In order to create change (the subject of Chapter 13), you will need to influence people to take action, and questions are one of the most effective ways to do this. After all, when are people more likely to take action—when they're *told* what to do, or when they come up with the ideas themselves in response to your carefully crafted questions? Questions help you elegantly direct the focus of those you want to influence.

Here are three examples of using questions to create change.

1. **A shift from "sugar water" to "changing the world."**

   A few years ago, one of the co-founders of Apple Computer, Steve Jobs, hired John Scully away from PepsiCo. At the time, Scully was a senior VP at PepsiCo and on the fast track to the top. Moreover, Apple was not doing very well financially and PepsiCo was doing fabulously. All the industry observers couldn't figure out how Steve got John to leave PepsiCo.

Here's how he did it. Steve met with John at Apple, showed him around, and discussed the Apple opportunity. At the end of the day, at just the right time, he asked John Scully one question: "Do you want to spend the rest of your life selling colored sugar water, or do you want a chance to change the world?" Then Steve shut up and waited for the question to really sink in.

It did. John answered, "I want a chance to change the world." It was the right question, asked in the right way, of the right person, at the right time, in the right place. It was the right question because Steve did his homework on John Scully. He knew that John was an intelligent, socially conscious person who wanted to make the world a better place to live. So his question brought up the pain of selling "colored sugar water" (not very intelligent and doesn't help the world) and the pleasure of "changing the world" (one of the things John wanted most in life). Steve also knew that John was a possibility person who was (and to this day is) intrigued by potential. John Scully doesn't want to get involved in sure things—in fact, he is drawn to the uncertain, which is why Steve asked, "Do you want a *chance* to change the world?"

You can do the same thing to get your point across. Ask people the questions that will get them to tell *themselves* the answer you want to hear! I teach programs to salespeople and managers on the art of asking action-producing questions. It's a powerful change skill that can be learned easily and quickly.

2. Questions access peak driver states which lead to peak performance.

I use questions extensively when I work with professional golfers because I know they need to be in a peak state to produce peak performance. First, we go out to the practice area, where I get them into a peak state by having them answer a series of questions, such as, "Do you remember the best round of golf you've played in the past three years? What course were you on? What kind of day was it? Who were you playing with? What score did you shoot? How were you walking down the fairway? How did you walk up to the ball and grip the club? How were you talking to yourself inside your head? How did it feel to be on a roll like that?"

As I ask those questions, I direct their mental pathway in a very specific way—to their resources—and their driver state changes. You can see it in the body. Then I have them walk up to the ball and swing. The vast majority of the time they hit the ball much farther and straighter than before. Their peak driver state leads to peak performance. It all starts with the questions I ask.

3. Use questions to get your kids to talk.

If it's a challenge to get your kids to talk, maybe you're just not asking the right questions. Let me give you an example. Say you just got home from work and want to find out about your child's day at school. Most parents ask the question, "What happened in school today?" Most kids answer, "Nothin'."

The problem is, this question is too general. It doesn't open up any specific files in your child's brain. Here are a couple of great file-opening questions:

1) *"What did you like best about school today?"* This will not only get your child to talk more, but it will train her to focus on the positives in her life.

2) *"Did you have any challenges today that I can help you with?"* This question trains her to look at her problems as challenges that will soon be solved with action.

What do you do if she answers, "I don't know"?
(I know your daughter would never say this, but I've
heard that other kids would!) Don't let her off the
hook—she knows the answer. When she says, "I don't
know," just shoot back with, "I know you don't know,
but if you did know, what would the answer be?" It's
amazing—it's much easier for her to come up with an
answer. Her brain goes "click," the files open up, and
she answers you about 80% of the time.

Let's say you're helping your daughter with her
homework. If she asks you a question and you believe
it's important for her to come up with her own answer,
just ask her something that directs her focus in the
appropriate way. If she asks, "How do you spell the
word *federal*?" just respond, "How would you spell
the first syllable in *federal*?" When she answers,
either correct her or say, "That's right! Now, how do
you spell the rest of the word?"

The bottom line when asking questions is this: **Know exactly
where you want the other person's mental focus to go, then ask
a question that will produce that focus.** Work backward from the
focus you want to create.

Section Three of this book is loaded with specific questions
you can use with yourself and others to effectively react to, anticipate,
create, and lead change in your life.

In the last two chapters, you've learned how managing the
emotions that drive your behavior will create the outcomes you want
in life. There are many ways you can change your emotions. What
do most people do when they want to feel better? All sorts of things,
such as take drugs, smoke cigarettes, eat, sleep, have sex, go shopping,
watch TV, exercise, etc. People do these things because they work.
Unfortunately, many of these behaviors have negative side effects, take
a lot of time, and/or are expensive.

You don't need to do any of the above. You now have two easy-to-use pathways you can turn to at any time to manage your driver states—the physical and mental pathways. These pathways are free, handy, and powerful. And you can use your newfound ability with questions to access these pathways in the blink of an eye. All you have to do is spend a few moments figuring out the pathways you use to access your most resourceful states, and duplicate them whenever you want to feel great!

Now let's apply the information in this chapter to your life by completing the Exercises for Action on the next page. Are you ready to begin to use questions more effectively now?

EXERCISES FOR ACTION

1. Make a copy of the Morning Questions and
    tape it somewhere (such as a mirror or the visor
    of your car) so you'll see it every morning. If you
    would like a copy of the Morning Questions
    printed on a sturdy card, please give my office
    a call at (800) 445–8183, extension 6290.

2. Make a copy of the Realignment Questions and put it
    in a place you can easily find in the heat of the moment.
    Whenever you find yourself in a painful situation, pull
    out the Questions and use them to change your state.

3. If you have kids, develop a few questions now that will
    enable them to create more resourceful answers in their
    lives. (This works with your spouse/significant other, too!)

4. If you work outside the home, develop a few questions that
    will enable your teammates at work to create more resource-
    ful answers in their lives.

In Chapter 1, you learned that the same set of beliefs and
strategies that has gotten you where you are now will not get you
where you want to go. You also learned you need to intelligently use
three different approaches to thrive in changing times:

*   **The Reactive Approach**
*   **The Anticipatory Approach**
*   **The Creative Approach**

Now you're ready to harness change on a whole new level! In the next section, you will learn the questions you need to answer and the strategies you must use to react to, anticipate, and create change in your personal and professional life.

Get ready to master . . .

Your Ultimate Change-Utilization Strategies!

Your Ultimate Change-Utilization Strategies

W e've covered a lot of material in a short period of time!
Let's take a moment now to review some of the key concepts.

Section One

- You can't just cope with change. You need to learn to use change to your advantage!

- Even in changing times, there is a set of principles and habits that you never want to change; and in changing times, the same set of beliefs and strategies that has gotten you where you are now will not get you where you want to go!

- **The Six Approaches to Change**

    1. Avoidance

    2. Resistance

    3. Apathy

    4. Reaction

    5. Anticipation

    6. Creation

Change Masters have numerous effective skills in each of the last three approaches.

- **Four Causes of Rapid Worldwide Change**

  1. Rapid improvements in technology

  2. Instantaneous worldwide communication

  3. Intense global competition

  4. Changing demographics and psychographics

- **Six Reasons to be Optimistic About the Future**

  1. A history of change

  2. Cultural diversity

  3. An increase in the number of democratic governments and free-market economies

  4. Multiple and abundant resources

  5. A booming economy

  6. The basic goodness of humanity

Section Two

- Principles and habits have the power to provide the solid foundation you need in our rapidly changing world.

- All changes in your environment are filtered through your beliefs.

- Your beliefs are the key element in the six-step belief cycle.

The Belief Cycle

- Mental creation precedes physical creation.

- **Six Thriving-on-Change Beliefs**

  1. Change equals opportunity.

  2. When things change, I must change!

  3. There is always a way to use change to my advantage.

  4. I'm going to enjoy my journey through this rapidly changing world.

  5. There is a life lesson to be learned from every change in my life.

  6. I'm an active participant in the change process!

- Use the Change Utilization Planner to create a plan to utilize any external change that occurs in your life.

- **Four Ways to Improve Your Strategies**
  1. Modeling
  2. Plussing
  3. Innovation
  4. Reinvention

- Use the Innovation Questions to generate thinking "outside the nine dots."

- Your driver states influence your actions. You can change driver states by changing your physical and mental pathways.

- **Five Essential Mental Focus Areas**
  1. Focus on outcomes first and process second.
  2. Selectively focus on the past, present, and future as needed.
  3. Focus on limitations and problems 2% of the time and resources and solutions 98% of the time.
  4. Focus on learning and growing.
  5. Focus on providing value.

- Use questions to direct your own or others' mental focus.

- **The Morning Questions**

  1. What am I happiest about in my life now?

  2. What am I most excited about in my life now?

  3. What am I most proud of in my life now?

  4. What am I most grateful for in my life now?

  5. What am I enjoying most in my life now?

  6. What am I most committed to in my life now?

  7. Who do I love? Who loves me?

- **The Realignment Questions**

  1. Concerning this situation, what possible information am I not currently aware of that would change how I feel about it?

  2. In addition to the meaning I'm currently attaching to the situation, what *else* could this mean?

  3. What could be the other person's "brain burp"?

  4. How unimportant will this be in five years?

  5. How can I change my physical and mental pathways *right now* to create a more resourceful driver state?

  6. In this resourceful driver state, what action could I take *right now* to clear up the misunderstanding?

Section Three

- Specific and powerful change strategies and how to apply them in three critical areas:

    1. Reacting to Change—Chapters 9, 10 and 11

    2. Anticipating Change—Chapter 12

    3. Creating Change—Chapter 13

- In Chapter 14, you will learn how to lead group change.

Get ready now to master your Ultimate Change-Utilization Strategies!

We'll begin by mastering the key strategies of successfully . . .

Reacting to Change: Letting Go of the Old

CHAPTER 9

Reacting to Change:
Letting Go of the Old

I was standing in the parking lot of Red Richie's Ford in Encinitas, California, talking to the car I had just traded in. With my hand resting on the hood, I said, "Well, old pal, it's time to say good-bye. We've had a lot of good times together, and I just want you to know how much I appreciate what you've done for me. I'm sure your new owner will take real good care of you. Thanks again." My old Jetta had 135,000 miles on it, and it had definitely seen better days. I'd just traded it in for a new car that was technologically superior. I should have been happy to get my new Continental, but instead, I felt sad.

What force can make a grown man talk to a car? That force is the subject of this chapter—Letting Go of the Old.

The key to change . . . is to let go of fear.

ROSEANNE CASH

Letting Go of the Old is the first stage of reacting to any change. As Paul Valéry said, "Every beginning is a consequence. Every beginning ends something." For me, the ending was selling my old car. To begin with a new car, I had to let go of the old. And, as silly as this example may seem, it illustrates my point: letting go can be tough. But Letting Go of the Old is the first stage in successfully reacting to any change.

The Three Stages of Change Reaction

Stage One—Letting Go of the Old

The starting point for all Change Reaction is the ending you must make to leave the old behind. Using the trapeze as a metaphor, you have to release the bar on which you're now swinging! For example, the people of South Africa first had to make the decision to let go of apartheid before they could move ahead and create a more inclusive government and society.

Stage Two—Transitioning Between the Old and the New

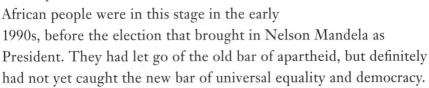

Transition is the period between the old and the new when you feel like you're in limbo. This is usually a time of great emotional intensity, but it's also the time when the greatest learning and growth can occur! Using the trapeze metaphor again, you're flying through the air between one trapeze and the other. The South African people were in this stage in the early 1990s, before the election that brought in Nelson Mandela as President. They had let go of the old bar of apartheid, but definitely had not yet caught the new bar of universal equality and democracy.

Stage Three—Embracing the New

The last stage in all Change Reaction is a new beginning. Your flight from one trapeze to the other is successful and you grab the new bar. For example, the South Africans will reach this stage when they establish a government where people of all races are represented equally.

Letting Go of the Old is the first—and often hardest—stage of Change Reaction. You're swinging from your "old" trapeze bar. You're comfortable; you've been swinging on it for years. You've learned to sit, hang, and throw your feet over the bar—you're the master of this environment. Now, however, external changes require you to move to a new bar, which has many advantages over the old one. Logically, you know that you should let go of the old bar so that you can swing over to the new; but emotionally, you don't want to let go. At the least, you have mixed feelings about it.

Almost anything is easier to get into than out of.

AGNES ALLEN

I received my dental degree in 1971. By 1974 I realized I absolutely hated practicing dentistry, and I had gotten into it for all the wrong reasons. However, it took me five years to finally let go of the old. Five years! Logically, I knew that dentistry wasn't for me, but emotionally I couldn't let go of the old because I started thinking things like:

- Man, I spent six years in pre-dentistry and dental school. It will all be wasted if I quit now!

- What will my parents, family, and friends think of me if I quit?

- What will I do for a living now?

- How will we maintain our lifestyle? This is the first time in my life I've ever made good money.

My thinking at that time was very typical of what many people go through when they're contemplating letting go of the old. This kind of thinking creates the three emotions that "super glue" people to their old trapeze bars:

- UNCERTAINTY—"The certainty of my present situation is better than the uncertainty that would be created when I let go."

- FEAR—"My present situation (even if it's painful) is better than the imagined pain of what will happen if I let go."

- REGRET—"It's too late to let go! I'm too old to let go! The world has changed too much for me to change now!" (These are what I call the "terrible too's" that block resourceful action.)

Do you remember learning about the power of questions in Chapter 8? Now you're going to use that power to help you let go of the old more easily. I've created an effective list of questions to help you handle changes in your life and in your business. The eight questions on the following pages are designed to move you through the self-imposed barriers of uncertainty, fear, and regret. They direct your mental focus toward your resources and solutions. I wish I had known how to ask these questions in 1974. I wouldn't have spent five years swinging on a bar I didn't belong on—making my life miserable for myself and those close to me!

You can use the following eight questions as soon as you identify any change in your personal life or business and want to react to it in the best possible manner. The main questions are listed first; under each main question are additional suggestions to help you come up with quality answers.

Study these questions carefully. They have real power to move you beyond your current situation to the future you were meant to have.

STAGE ONE

Questions for Letting Go of the Old

1. What, precisely, is the external change?

Describe the external change in factual, logical terms. Leave your emotional reaction aside.

- Are there any secondary changes this external change might produce? What else might occur for myself or others due to this external change?

2. **As a result of this external change, what is changing for me whether I like it or not?**

   Denial doesn't work. Acknowledge the losses to yourself and others, and openly discuss your losses with people who care about you.

   - What, if anything, am I losing?
   - What, if anything, am I gaining?

3. **Despite this external change, what *isn't* changing for me?**

   In times of change, it's easy to focus on your losses and overlook your resources and the things you still have in your life that should be appreciated. To get an objective view, you might find it helpful to talk with friends or colleagues.

   - What is staying the same?
   - What resources do I still have?
   - Who can I count on in this time of external change?

4. **Why do I think the external change happened?**

   Sometimes coming up with a reason makes us more accepting of the change. If you can't come up with a reason, you may have to turn to your faith in a higher power or whatever you believe in.

   - Was it a change in the economy, the world, or another person? Were there circumstances beyond my control that contributed to this change?
   - What part, if any, did I play in the creation of the external change?

5. **What does this external change mean to me?**

There are many possible meanings for any change. Brainstorm a list, and then choose one that empowers you to be, do, have, and give more.

6. **Why is it important for me to accept this change now?**

If you have a strong enough "why," you'll figure out how you need to change.

- In the long run, what will it cost me if I continue to hang on to the old?

- In the long run, what will I gain when I let go and move ahead?

7. **How can I mark the end of the old to let myself and everyone else know I'm moving on?**

It's an important part of the process of change to recognize the passing of one era and the beginning of another. To mark this change, create a ritual or do something that has meaning for you.

8. **What can I do immediately or in the near future to utilize this change to my advantage?**

Action is power! Decide upon something you can do immediately or as soon as possible to move ahead in a new direction.

- What is my plan to use this change to help me learn and grow?

- What action will I take first? Second? Third?

- How will I recognize and celebrate my progress as I keep moving forward?

These questions are equally effective for both personal and professional transitions. I used these questions recently to help a good friend of mine deal with a significant change: moving to a new city as the result of her husband's job transfer. She gave me permission to share our conversation because it was so helpful to her. On the next pages you'll see how I took her through each question and what her responses were.

Letting Go of the Old in Your Personal Life

QUESTION 1

What, precisely, is the external change?

••

MY WORDS

Sue, tell me in your own words exactly what the change is. Be as objective as possible. What's true about this external change?

RESPONSE

The external change is a promotion for my husband that requires our family to move 1,500 miles away from our current home.

QUESTION 2

As a result of this external change, what is changing for me whether I like it or not?

....

MY WORDS

Now, Sue, tell me: What are you losing as a result of your move?

RESPONSE

We won't be living in the home we've owned for eight years.We'll be losing the almost daily personal contact we've had with our neighbors. The two kids won't be going to the only school they've ever attended. We'll be losing all the support services (bank, pediatrician, supermarket, auto repair shop) we've established here. We'll be moving 1,500 miles away from my parents, so we won't see them as often.

MY WORDS

Sue, this may sound strange and you may have to think about it some, but what, if anything, are you gaining from this transition?

RESPONSE

Well, we will be gaining a new home that is newer and bigger than our old one. We'll be gaining a new set of neighbors, and we can still come back and see our old friends a couple of times a year. We'll be living in an area that has a lot more recreational opportunities. The kids will be gaining a wonderful new school and a new set of friends. Our family income will be going up about 15% and our expenses will actually drop. My husband will be gaining the promotion he's been working hard to get. Our new home is very near a university, and I'm considering going back to school to get my master's degree.

QUESTION 3

Despite this external change, what isn't changing for me?

MY WORDS

Sue, what will still be the same in your life after the move? What isn't changing?

RESPONSE

We'll still have our friends here—it's not like we'll never talk to or see them again. We still have our parents and their love and support. We still have our health. You know, most importantly, we still have each other as a family. We still have our memories of our life here in San Diego.

MY WORDS

What resources do you have that you can draw upon right now?

RESPONSE

We still have our financial resources. Bill's company is paying for all the costs associated with the move. We have the support of our families and friends.

MY WORDS

Who can you count on in this time of external change?

RESPONSE

We can count on each other to help everyone through this challenging time. We can count on my family; my best friend, Mina; my boss at work—she's already told me to take the week off so I can make all the arrangements; my friend, Larry—he's a lawyer and he can advise us on some of the legal stuff. In fact, I have a lot of friends I can call upon to help out.

Why do I think the external change happened?

MY WORDS

Why did your husband get promoted, which requires a family move?

RESPONSE

Bill is a very hard-working, intelligent, team playing kind of a guy. This isn't his first or last promotion. He's working hard for a company that's growing rapidly.

MY WORDS

What part did you play in creating the move?

RESPONSE

The part I played in all this is I agreed to the move after Bill and I talked about all the pros and cons. I also married a guy I knew would progress a long way in a company with operations all over the world.

QUESTION 5

What does this external change mean to me?

MY WORDS

Sue, I'd like you to take a few minutes and think of all the possible things, good and bad, this move could mean to you. Just let yourself come up with everything it could mean. I'm going to write them all down.

RESPONSE

There are many things this change could mean. It could mean that we will never be happy as a family again. This move could mean lots of pain and heartache for everyone involved as things slowly get back to normal.

It could also mean a brand-new start. It could mean an expansion of our circle of friends and our opportunities, rather than a loss. This move could be just another one of life's changes. A change that will help us all learn and grow.

MY WORDS

Sue, out of this list, which is the meaning you want to focus on?

RESPONSE

I'm going to focus on the last two meanings. This move is an expansion and a learning experience in flexibility for the kids and myself!

QUESTION 6

Why is it important for me to accept this change now?

....

MY WORDS

Sue, why must you accept this change now? What will it cost you if you don't accept the move?

RESPONSE

It's important for me to accept this change now because if I don't, the whole family will suffer. It's important for me to set a good example for the kids, to help them through this time. They're not exactly thrilled about moving right now.

MY WORDS

What will you gain by accepting this change?

RESPONSE

I'll gain peace of mind that we're doing the right thing. I'll gain a greater sense of control over my life. I'll gain the perspective I need to make the move as pleasurable as a long-distance move can be.

QUESTION 7

How can I mark the end of the old to let myself and everyone else know I'm moving on?

MY WORDS

Sue, it's important to recognize the ending of something so we can move on. How do you want to mark this transition in your life?

RESPONSE

You know what? This move is just the beginning of another chapter in our lives. We can mark the end of the old chapter by having a huge appreciation party at our home to thank all of the people who have made our life here so special.

What can I do immediately or in the near future to utilize this change to my advantage?

MY WORDS

So, what's your plan of action, Sue? How are you going to use this change to learn and grow?

RESPONSE

Well, first I'm going to sit down with the whole family and ask them some of the questions you've just asked me. Then we're going to set up a schedule of everything that needs to be done before the move and who is going to do what. This will be a great practical exercise for all of us in taking a big job down to bite-sized chunks that we can actually swallow.

MY WORDS

That's great, Sue! Now the last question: How are you going to recognize and celebrate your progress as you keep moving forward?

RESPONSE

We're going to have weekly family meetings to see how we're doing and revise our plan if necessary. After we've moved, we're going to invite Bill's and my parents and a couple of our best friends to our new home!

Do you see the power of these questions? Did you notice how Sue became more and more resourceful as we went along? She always had the resources within her—she just hadn't tapped them because she hadn't asked these resource-releasing questions.

This is a good time to mention that you shouldn't make every change you're considering. Sometimes it's best not to change. These eight questions will help you determine whether the change is right for you or not.

Now, let's answer the same eight questions for an external change in the business world. The example we will use is a change affecting many of my corporate clients—consumer demand for higher quality and lower cost products and services, along with heavy competition in a global marketplace to provide those products and services at the lowest possible price.

"Mike" is a composite of a number of people I've worked with who are experiencing change in their businesses.

Letting Go of the Old in Your Business

QUESTION 1

What, precisely, is the external change?

MY WORDS

Mike, tell me precisely, what is the biggest change affecting your company?

RESPONSE

Our customers are demanding higher quality/lower cost products and services. Our worldwide competition is, in many cases, doing a better job of providing these products and services than we are.

QUESTION 2

As a result of this external change, what is changing for us?

••

MY WORDS

What has your company lost as a result of this change?

RESPONSE

Our market share was down 7% last quarter, our income was off 2%, and our expenses haven't changed. We've lost numerous customers to our competitors. After twelve years of steady growth, we seem to have lost our vitality. Our people are getting a little discouraged and there's lots of finger-pointing.

MY WORDS

Mike, I know this sounds strange, but how is your company possibly going to benefit from this change? What will you gain?

RESPONSE

We're getting a chance to really examine everything we do. We were getting a little complacent, just making small improvements. Now we have to take a look at absolutely everything, with an eye toward making massive improvements.

Despite this external change, what isn't changing for us?

MY WORDS

Mike, in spite of this change, what's staying the same for your company?

RESPONSE

We're still number one in market share in our industry. We still have our reputation for excellent quality and service.

MY WORDS

What resources do you still have?

RESPONSE

We have over 21,000 active customers. We have the financial resources needed to make the changes.

MY WORDS

Who can you count on in this time of external change?

RESPONSE

We have 350 dedicated employees. We have our vendors, who have a vested interest in our success. We also have two consultants who are extremely helpful.

QUESTION 4

Why do we think the external change happened?

MY WORDS

Mike, why do you think this external change occurred?

RESPONSE

The change happened because there is a growing trend toward value in the marketplace today. New technology has made it easier for our competitors to produce higher quality products and services at lower costs. New worldwide competitors are entering the marketplace every month.

QUESTION 5

What does this external change mean to us?

MY WORDS

Mike, take a few minutes and think of all the possible meanings this change could have for your company.

RESPONSE

It means we've been resting on our laurels. We haven't listened to our customers as well as we should have. We haven't put enough of our resources into R&D to improve product quality, and it means we'll have to decrease our cost of doing business as we increase quality. This external change is a wake-up call to alert us that we have to make some internal changes. It means strong competition makes everyone better.

MY WORDS

And which meaning do you want to focus on?

RESPONSE

We're going to take it as a wake-up call that will give us a chance to be stronger and more competitive.

QUESTION 6

Why is it important for us to change now?

MY WORDS

What will it cost if your company doesn't change now?

RESPONSE

If we don't make these changes now, our market share and bottom line will continue to decline. We'll continue to lose valuable customers, and we may lose some of our employees to our competitors, which means our morale will continue to go downhill. If we don't make some changes now, our company may not be around in five years.

MY WORDS

How can your company gain by making these changes now?

RESPONSE

We can quite possibly come up with ways we never would have thought of before to increase our market share and profitability. We can involve all our employees in the process and create a stronger team than ever before. Best of all, if we learn to overcome this challenge now we can handle challenges like it in the years to come, so we never find ourselves in this kind of spot again!

QUESTION 7

How can we mark the end of the old to let people know we're moving on?

MY WORDS

Mike, how can your company mark the end of the old way of doing things so your people will truly understand you're serious about making these changes?

RESPONSE

Lee Iacocca did it by calling his company "The New Chrysler." We can call a meeting next week of all the employees to let them know exactly what is going on and to ask them for input on a plan of action. We can let our customers know about our new "Partners in Success" program.

QUESTION 8

What can we do immediately or in the near future to utilize this change to our advantage?

MY WORDS

Mike, what's your action plan to use this change to move ahead?

RESPONSE

We can do a better job of polling our customers to discover their unique challenges. We can look for ways to improve the quality of our products and services. We can also look for ways to cut costs. This may include developing more efficient processes and better utilization of new technology. We may have to reduce the number of people on our team. We can look for all the ways to do more with less. I'm going to call a meeting today at two o'clock to develop a preliminary plan of action!

MY WORDS

How are you and your company going to recognize and celebrate your progress as you keep moving forward?

RESPONSE

We're going to set benchmarks for ourselves and check in on a regular basis, at least weekly. Every time we achieve a production or sales goal, we're going to let the whole company know and reward the responsible players with a special lunch or party. And if we continually meet our goals for the next six months, everyone and their families will get a trip to Disneyland!

Imagine Mike's emotional state and plan of action before answering the eight Letting Go of the Old questions. Now, imagine his emotional state and plan of action after he answered the questions. There's a substantial difference, right? After only eight simple questions!

One very powerful reason people have trouble letting go of the old is their fear of the next stage of Change Reaction, Transitioning Between the Old and the New. You've probably heard of battered-spouse syndrome, where people stay in a relationship even though they are being physically abused. Often, they are more afraid of what will happen if they leave the relationship than they are hurt by the abuse they are enduring today. The certain pain of the present is less severe than the imagined pain of the future. It's all too easy for someone on the outside to say, "Just leave!" But have you ever stayed in a bad situation longer than you should have? The same fear was probably present in your life at that time.

One doesn't discover new lands without consenting

to lose sight of the shore for a very long time.

ANDRÉ GIDE

In this chapter, you learned eight essential questions you can ask that will create the answers you need to let go of the old successfully. In the next chapter, you will learn seven questions that will guide you through Stage Two of Change Reaction, Transitioning Between the Old and the New. But before you read on, apply what you learned in this chapter to your life by completing the Exercises for Action beginning on the next page!

EXERCISES FOR ACTION

1. Isolate one change you are experiencing in your personal life right now. Answer the following Letting Go of the Old questions concerning this personal change.

   A. What, precisely, is the external change?

   - Are there any secondary changes that this external change might produce? What else might occur for myself or for others due to this external change?

   B. As a result of this external change, what is changing for me whether I like it or not?

   - What, if anything, am I losing?

   - What, if anything, am I gaining?

   C. Despite this external change, what isn't changing for me?

   - What is staying the same?

   - What resources do I still have?

   - Who can I count on in this time of external change?

   D. Why do you think the external change happened?

   - Was it a change in the economy, the world, or another person? Were there circumstances beyond my control that contributed to this change?

   - What part, if any, did you play in the creation of the external change?

   E. What does this external change mean to me?

F. Why is it important for me to accept this change now?

- In the long run, what will it cost me if I continue to hang on to the old?

- In the long run, what will I gain when I let go and move ahead?

G. How can I mark the end of the old to let myself and everyone else know I'm moving on?

H. What can I do immediately or in the near future to utilize this change to my advantage?

- What is my plan to use this change to help me learn and grow?

- What action will I take first? Second? Third?

- How will I recognize and celebrate my progress as I keep moving forward?

2. Isolate one change you are experiencing in your business or professional life right now. Answer the following Letting Go of the Old questions concerning this business change.

A. What, precisely, is the external change?

- Are there any secondary changes that this external change might produce? What else might occur for myself, for others, or for my business due to this external change?

B. As a result of this external change, what is changing whether we like it or not?

- What, if anything, are we losing?

- What, if anything, are we gaining?

C. Despite this external change, what isn't changing?

- What is staying the same?

- What resources do we still have?

- Who can we count on in this time of external change?

D. Why do we think the external change happened?

- Was it a change in the economy, the world, another business? Were there circumstances beyond our control that contributed to this change?

- What part, if any, did we play in the creation of the external change?

E. What does this external change mean to us?

F. Why is it important for us to accept this change now?

- In the long run, what will it cost us if we continue to hang on to the old?

- In the long run, what will we gain when we let go and move ahead?

G. How can we mark the end of the old to let ourselves and everyone else know we're moving on?

H. What can we do immediately or in the near future to utilize this change to our advantage?

- What is our plan to use this change to help us learn and grow?

- What action will we take first? Second? Third?

- How will we recognize and celebrate our progress as we keep moving forward?

Now that you've resourcefully let go of the old bar, it's time for the exciting flight through the air! Read on to learn how to soar with confidence, elegance, and competence!

Discover how to master . . .

Transitioning Between the Old and the New!

Reacting to Change: Transitioning Between the Old and the New

Right now, think of a time in your life when you were in transition—moving from high school to college or from high school to your first job, moving from one city to another, moving from one relationship to another, or moving from one job to another. Go back to that time in your life and experience it now. What pictures are popping into your mind? What words were you saying to yourself then? How did it feel, and what words did you use to describe that feeling? Experience it now the same way you did then!

If you're like most people in transition, it was probably an exciting, tension-packed, maybe even scary time. That's just the way transitions are between the old and new!

It's not so much that we're afraid of change

or so in love with the old ways,

but it's that place in between that we fear.

It's like being between two trapezes.

It's Linus when his blanket is in the dryer.

There is nothing to hold on to.

MARILYN FERGUSON

When I made the transition out of dentistry in 1979, I felt lost for about a year and a half—I had no clear idea of what to do with my life. So my family and I moved back to my hometown. I took a few college courses in a wide variety of fields with no real purpose in mind. I helped my wife get her own business started; I got into woodworking, which I had never done before. I also began running marathons. During one period, I was putting in over one hundred training miles a week! While that may be admirable, in my situation it wasn't healthy. Looking back on it now, I was a 32-year-old guy whose blanket was in the dryer, and I didn't know what to do in the meantime!

In Stage Two of Change Reaction, Transitioning Between the Old and the New, it's as if you're flying through the air between two trapezes. Is this a time of intense internal change? Absolutely! Is this a time of high levels of emotion? Probably! Is this a time of extreme uncertainty, fear, and inaction, or a time of intense creativity and innovation? That depends upon how you approach it. The purpose of this chapter is to help you learn how to use this transition period as a time of high-level creativity, innovation, and discovery.

South Africa began this transitional stage in 1990 when the government of F. W. De Klerk made a historic decision to abandon its decades-old policy of apartheid. With the election of Nelson Mandela and the government of national unity in 1994, South Africans let go of the old, but as of 1996 they still haven't fully caught the bar in many areas. (Many of the schools are still segregated, massive inequities between black and white still exist, and the entire country is struggling to find a new balance both socially and economically.) It is a time of great uncertainty, as demonstrated by the militant political movements of both left and right.

In the transition between the old and the new, people and programs that promise a return to the "good old days" may be very appealing. You saw this in the 1995 elections in Poland, when President Lech Walesa was replaced by Aleksander Kwasniewski, a Communist. In times of transition, uncertainty can take over and paralyze you. It is absolutely critical that you create your *own* certainty in this stage, with a 100%, no-holds-barred belief in your ability to catch the new bar. Great leaders can do this for an entire nation. Winston Churchill and Franklin Delano Roosevelt did it for Britain and the United States during World War II. That's what Mandela is attempting to do for South Africa.

In this stage, old weaknesses that you've been living with for a while may emerge. I've seen this happen both in people's personal lives and in corporate cultures. The structure and routine of swinging on the old trapeze bonds people and processes together. When the glue is gone, weaknesses can appear. However, this has its advantages in the long run, because when weaknesses become apparent, then you can correct them.

The transition stage can also be a time of colossal creativity, innovation, discovery, and progress because you have far fewer attachments. This is why outsiders often can create breakthroughs, because they look at things with "detached eyes." The greatest opportunity for growth is in the transition stage. This opportunity needs to be nurtured. That is exactly what you will learn to do in this chapter!

Chaos often breeds life, while order breeds habit.

HENRY ADAMS

Just as there were questions to assist you in letting go of the old, there are questions to help make the transition between old and new easier and more creative. Think of one of the changes you used in last chapter's "Exercises for Action" as you read and answer the following questions.

STAGE TWO
Questions for Transitioning Between the Old and the New

1. **What are some of the limiting, unwritten rules I can break? And/or, what are some of the written rules I can change?**

   Remember what you learned in Chapter 6: To be an innovator, you need to break unwritten rules and/or change written ones.

2. **What opportunities are available to me now that I've let go of the old?**

   Brainstorm a list of ways you can expand your horizons in this time of change.

3. **What are some new ideas I can use in making the transition?**

   Consider all the possibilities you created in questions 1 and 2, and look at everything in a new light. Where can you go to discover others' ideas you can model?

- Ask, "Why does it have to be this way?" and "Why not try it this way?"

- What analogies and metaphors could you use to suggest a new way of looking at the change?

4. **What temporary support systems can I utilize or create? What relationships can I strengthen as a result of this change?**

   This is a great time to seek out people who will support you and who will allow you to support them. This is not the time to be around people who might bring you down. Find and nurture relationships that empower you!

5. **How will I constructively fill the space left by the old?**

   During transitional times, it's important to create satisfying, empowering alternatives to replace what's being left behind.

   - Ask, "What will be gone from my life that I need to replace?"

   - For each element that is disappearing, come up with at least two ways for you to get the same feelings and results by doing something else. Make sure your alternatives are empowering!

6. **What will I do to stay healthy during this time of transition?**

   Take care of yourself! Times of transition can bring great opportunity and also great stress. It's vital to make sure you eat well, exercise regularly, get adequate sleep, and take breaks by doing something for pure pleasure.

   - Ask, "How can I use this opportunity to create even more balance in my life?"

7. In what ways will I continue to focus on the new?

Even if you find yourself doing a few somersaults between trapezes, it's important to keep your focus firmly on where you're going! Ask yourself the following questions:

- How great will I feel once this transition is completed and I've made it to the other side?

- What enormous benefits await me and the people I care about?

- What do I need to do next to keep the process of change moving along?

I used these transition questions when I spoke to my friend Sue about her move. Here's how our conversation went.

Stage Two: Questions for Transitioning Between the Old and the New in Your Personal Life

QUESTION 1

What are some limiting unwritten rules I can break? And/or what are some written rules I can change?

MY WORDS

Sue, as you think about this move, what are some limiting unwritten or written rules you can break that will make this move easier?

RESPONSE

A limiting unwritten rule we can break is the one that says moving has to be a long, unpleasant experience for everyone involved—especially for the mom of the family. We're going to spread the responsibilities as evenly as possible among all family members as we make this an exciting time for everyone. There are also some written rules at Mike's company that make it tough on families like ours. One of those rules involves the limited amount of time employees get off for a move. We're going to see if we can get it extended by three days.

QUESTION 2

What opportunities are available to me now that I've let go of the old?

MY WORDS

What are the opportunities awaiting you as you make this transition?

RESPONSE

I've never really thought about it, but there are some great opportunities here. Now that we're moving to Denver, we can do more hiking, skiing, and mountain biking. We can decorate our home the way I've always wanted to—we actually have the money to do it this time. With our increased income, I can get some help with the house so I'll have more time for graduate school. We can also use this experience as an opportunity to become closer as a family.

Q U E S T I O N   3

What are some new ideas I can use in making this transition?

MY WORDS

Sue, what are some of your ideas about this move that will make it easier and more pleasant for you and your family? What possibilities can you consider in a new light?

RESPONSE

My friend, Joyce, moved a year ago, and her family seemed to react well. I'm going to give her a call. One new idea I know I'm going to use is to let go of my total responsibility for the move. I'm going to let the movers do almost all the packing, and I'm going to involve the whole family in planning and implementing this move!

MY WORDS

What are some analogies and metaphors that will help you suggest a new way to regard this transition?

RESPONSE

There are a couple of metaphors we can all use to feel more resourceful. One is, this move is just the end of one chapter and the beginning of another. The other is, we're starting another leg on our journey together as a family.

QUESTION 4

What temporary support systems can I utilize or create, and what relationships can I strengthen?

MY WORDS

It's an excellent idea to be with people who will support you and allow you to support them. Now is the time to enhance the relationships that empower you! Who can you call upon to support you now?

RESPONSE

I'm going to use the moving company's services to the fullest. My mom and dad have offered to watch the kids during the moving process; I'm going to take them up on that. Joyce has offered to help, so I'm going to ask her to lend a hand when I need it—and go to lunch with her when I need a break! Mike's company also has a comprehensive relocation service package. I'm going to use it to the max.

QUESTION 5

How will I constructively fill the space left by the old?

MY WORDS

Sue, now's the time to take a look at the things you'll be losing as a result of this move, so you can discover creative ways to get the same (or similar) feelings by doing or having something else. How can you create balance in your life and the lives of your family?

RESPONSE

One thing that will be partially gone is the almost weekly face-to-face contact we had with my parents. We can fill that space by coming back to San Diego at least twice a year. My folks have already said they want to come out to see us two or three times a year as well. In addition, there are several retired people in our new neighborhood. We can become good friends with them.

Another space that will be created is our relationship with our friends. But we'll be coming back to see our "old" friends twice a year and they're always welcome to come see us. And we'll make lots of new friends in Denver—in the neighborhood, at Mike's work, through the clubs and organizations we'll join. We'll especially make sure the kids make lots of new contacts. They're worried about having new friends.

Another space that will be created is the network of services we have here—dentist, doctor, cleaners, etc. Mike's relocation service can provide assistance in this area, and I'm good at asking neighbors who they recommend.

QUESTION 6

What will I do to stay healthy during this stage?

MY WORDS

Sue, it's especially important to eat well, exercise regularly, get adequate sleep, and occasionally take revitalizing "time outs" as you make this transition. How are you going to take care of yourself?

RESPONSE

I'm not going to get all wrapped up in the move this time. I'm going to keep walking with Joyce each morning until the move. I'm going to look for a new walking buddy as soon as I get to Denver. I'm going to keep eating well and arrange things so I don't get overloaded. We're going to keep Sunday as a family day where we just do fun things together.

QUESTION 7

In what ways will I continue to focus on the new?

MY WORDS

Even if you're doing a few somersaults on your transitional flight, it's important to focus on the new bar at all times. What are you going to focus on for the next few weeks?

RESPONSE

It will really be nice to move into our wonderful new home. Denver is a great place to raise a family, and I'm excited about all the new possibilities. There are excellent financial benefits as a result of the move. The kids will love our new home with its huge lot. I know Mike will love his new job! I need to keep focusing on all the benefits of the move and following the plan we created here.

When leaves change and fall,

fertile soil is created and the heavens are revealed.

NATE BOOTH

In the last chapter, we looked at the example of a business change where consumer demand for higher-quality, lower-cost products and services as well as increased competition was causing Mike's company to make a transition. Here are the results of using the Transitioning Between the Old and the New questions with Mike.

Stage Two: Questions for Transitioning Between the Old and the New in Your Business

QUESTION 1

What are some limiting unwritten rules that we can break? And/or what are some written rules we can change?

MY WORDS

Mike, every corporation has unwritten and written rules. But to be an innovator, you need to break and/or change them. What unwritten or written rules are you prepared to break and/or change?

RESPONSE

Because of our past successes, we have unwritten rules that say we never reduce the cost of our products and services, and we never reduce the number of employees. We will have to break these two unwritten rules now.

We also have an unwritten rule in our company that says it takes twelve months of R&D to create a new product. We're going to do a better job in six months this time. And we have several written rules in our policy and procedures manual that severely limit our people in the R&D process. We're going to change those rules.

QUESTION 2

What opportunities are available to us now that we've let go of the old?

MY WORDS

Mike, what opportunities are you ready to take advantage of now that you're in a time of transition?

RESPONSE

We have the opportunity to create more innovative products and services. We have the opportunity to look at our entire R&D process so we can become more flexible and provide a faster turnaround. We have the opportunity to re-engineer our entire company to improve efficiency and cut costs.

QUESTION 3

What are some new ideas we can use in making this transition?

....

MY WORDS

Consider your company's possibilities in a new light. This is a great time to ask "why" and "why not." I suggest you look for analogies and metaphors that suggest a new way of thinking. What if you had a brainstorming session to generate a huge list of possibilities?

RESPONSE

We've never gone to anyone outside the company to help us in times of change before, but I know one of our vendors has successfully gone through a similar process. I'm going to give them a call and set up a brainstorming session.

We're also going to create product/service development teams like Ford did with their two Taurus projects. We're going to actively solicit ideas from all our employees.

We can use the metaphor of a journey between our old and new product development processes to symbolize this transitional phase.

QUESTION 4

What temporary support systems can we utilize or create, and what relationships can we strengthen?

MY WORDS

How are you and your team going to support each other and foster the relationships that empower you as a company and as individuals?

RESPONSE

Let's use that consulting firm Martha told us about and create a corporate team to spearhead our change process. Let's thoroughly communicate with all our associates to make everyone a partner in our progress.

QUESTION 5

How will we constructively fill the space left by the old?

MY WORDS

You need to take a look at what you're losing as a result of this change so you can discover creative ways to get the same (or similar) results by doing or having something else.

RESPONSE

We need to replace the revenue we've lost. We're doing extremely well with Products D and E right now. We will step up our marketing and sales efforts with them. And we need to enhance the team cohesion and confidence that has dissipated over the last few quarters. We'll involve employees on all levels of the company in this effort to re-engineer ourselves.

QUESTION 6

What will we do to stay healthy during this time of transition?

MY WORDS

How is everyone involved in this transition going to take care of their physical health during this time of transition and additional stress?

RESPONSE

We're probably all going to have some challenges in the months ahead. It will probably mean longer office hours for many of us. Let's keep our exercise programs in gear, continue to eat healthfully, keep a positive attitude, and encourage everyone to do the same. Maybe once a quarter we'll treat everyone to a company-wide "Celebrate Our Successes" lunch!

QUESTION 7

In what ways will we continue to focus on the new?

MY WORDS

Finally, how will you keep the entire company focused on the results of successfully managing this transition?

RESPONSE

We can openly and vigorously communicate to all our people what the new company will be like. We will talk about our progress at every meeting we have. When our prototype product/service is created, we will have a model of it shown/demonstrated to all our people.

Answering these seven questions is extremely important to your success in Stage Two of Change Reaction, Transitioning Between the Old and the New. If you don't, your focus may go back to the old bar, or you may focus on the ground below and get caught up in "the pain of it all." These seven questions will keep your focus where it belongs—on resources, solutions, and the future you will create!

Now let's apply these seven questions to a change in your personal or professional life by completing the Exercises for Action on the following pages.

EXERCISES FOR ACTION

1. Use the same personal change you selected in the Exercises for Action in the last chapter. The seven Questions for Transitioning Between the Old and the New questions listed below will help you develop a plan for this stage.

   1. **What are some of the limiting, unwritten rules I can break? And/or what are some of the written rules I can change?**

   2. **What opportunities are available to me now that I've let go of the old?**

   3. **What are some new ideas I can use in making the transition?**
      - Ask, "Why does it have to be this way?" and "Why not try it this way?"
      - What analogies and metaphors could you use to suggest a new way of looking at the change?

   4. **What temporary support systems can I utilize or create? What relationships can I strengthen as a result of this change?**

   5. **How will I constructively fill the space left by the old?**
      - Ask, "What will be gone from my life that I need to replace?"
      - For each element that is disappearing, come up with at least two ways for you to get the same feelings and results by doing something else. Make sure your alternatives are empowering!

6. **What will I do to stay healthy during this time of transition?**

   - Ask, "How can I use this opportunity to create even more balance in my life?"

7. **In what ways will I continue to focus on the new? Ask yourself the following questions:**

   - How great will I feel once this transition is completed and I've made it to the other side?

   - What enormous benefits await me and the people I care about?

   - What do I need to do next to keep the process of change moving along?

2. For the same business change that you selected in the Exercises for Action in the last chapter, use the seven Questions for Transitioning Between the Old and the New listed below to develop a plan for this stage.

   1. **What are some of the limiting, unwritten rules we can break? And/or what are some of the written rules we can change?**

   2. **What opportunities are available to us now that we've let go of the old?**

   3. **What are some new ideas we can use in making the transition?**

      - Ask, "Why does it have to be this way?" and "Why not try it this way?"

      - What analogies and metaphors could you use to suggest a new way of looking at the change?

4. **What temporary support systems can we utilize or create? What relationships can we strengthen as a result of this change?**

5. **How will we constructively fill the space left by the old?**

   - Ask, "What will be gone from our lives that we need to replace?"

   - For each element that is disappearing, come up with at least two ways for you to get the same feelings and results by doing something else. Make sure your alternatives are empowering!

6. **What will we do to stay healthy during this time of transition?**

   - Ask, "How can we use this opportunity to create even more balance in our lives?"

7. **In what ways will we continue to focus on the new? Ask the following questions:**

   - How great will we feel once this transition is completed and we've made it to the other side?

   - What enormous benefits await us and the people we care about?

   - What do we need to do next to keep the process of change moving along?

In the last chapter, you let go of the old trapeze. In this chapter, you flew through the air between the old and the new with the greatest of ease. In the next chapter, Embracing the New, you finally have the pleasure of catching the new bar. The applause of the crowd awaits you!

Turn the page to experience the joys of . . .

Embracing the New!

CHAPTER 11

Reacting to Change: Embracing the New

The only joy in the world is to begin.

CESARE PAVESE

If reacting to change begins with an ending, it must end with a beginning. The beginning, using our trapeze metaphor, is catching the new bar. Correctly going through the first two stages, (Letting Go of the Old and Transitioning Between the Old and the New), puts you in perfect position to grab the new bar. In reality, embracing the new is the easiest part of the change reaction process—if you've done your job in the first two stages and you're focused on your goal.

Catching the new bar can sometimes be a challenge. Why?

- You may still be thinking about the past and looking back at the old bar.

- You may be focusing on what you are afraid of and looking down at the ground.

- You may be remembering the pain of past failures and have your eyes closed.

- You may be trying to hold on to both bars simultaneously— which can't be done!

Obviously, none of these are the best strategies for catching the trapeze successfully! You want to have your eyes open and focused on the new bar. After you catch the trapeze, you can then make it your own.

Remember, beginnings are often messy. It's like the first few dozen times you attempted to tie your shoes. You got the job done but it took forever. You had to use all your concentration to do it, and you ended up with a messy knot. But beginnings are also joyful, because you're the happiest when you're learning and growing. A growing plant is "new" every hour. A growing person is, too!

In my own journey from leaving my career as a dentist to creating a new life for myself and my family, after a long and somersault-filled transition stage I finally embraced the new when I made the decision to go back to college and earn a master's degree in counseling. I became focused on the bar of wanting to help people move toward their goals and enjoy the process. I earned my degree in 1983.

Below is a mental exercise you can use as you create your new beginning. You will use this exercise again in the Stage Three Questions later in this chapter. Read the exercise all the way through first, then put the book down and do it.

The Mental Creation Exercise

1. Think of an area in your life where you need to make a new beginning. (Hint: You can use the personal or business situation from the Exercises for Action in Chapters 9 and 10.)

2. Stand with your eyes closed. Put your whole body in a resourceful physiology—erect posture, head slightly up, breathing deeply.

3. Remember a specific time in the past when you felt strong, powerful, and confident.

4. Experience that time all over again. Breathe the way you were breathing then. Create big, bright, colorful pictures of that time in your mind. Hear all the same sounds around you. Repeat what you were saying to yourself then. Feel throughout your entire body the exhilaration you felt. See, hear, and feel the experience all over again.

5. Now, intensify the experience by about 20%. Go for it! Good! Intensify the experience *another* 20%! Excellent!

6. Now, in this state, mentally experience yourself "grabbing the new bar"—embracing a new beginning in the area you want to change. Feel the thrill of this new beginning throughout your entire body!

7. Do the above six steps over and over until this feeling becomes a natural part of you.

Here are three powerful questions that will assist you in catching the new bar.

Stage Three

Questions for Embracing the New

1. What can I do first that will be easy to accomplish, and will help me to embrace the new?

Give yourself the boost of immediate success by picking a few easy things to do first.

2. How specifically will I celebrate my successes along the way?

Make sure you give yourself rewards as you make the changes in your life. Remember, you deserve it!

3. How will I keep moving toward my dreams, using all the resources this new beginning provides?

Have a game plan for how you will use what you're learning and accomplishing during this new stage of your life to progress toward your ultimate dreams. Keep the vision of your dreams in front of you—it will make your journey more exciting and fun.

Let's continue with the same personal and business examples we used in Chapters 9 and 10. By the time I asked the following questions, Sue was feeling pretty good about the impending move to Denver—in her mind, she had already incorporated the change into her life. Her answers to the Questions for Embracing the New gave her even more clarity, and helped her create a plan for the time following the move.

Stage Three: Questions for Embracing The New In Your Personal Life

QUESTION 1

What can I do first that will be easy to accomplish and will help me to embrace the new?

MY WORDS

Sue, one of the best ways to embrace the new is to create a few easy successes for yourself right away. What are you going to do first that will be easy to accomplish?

RESPONSE

We're going to take it easy when we get to Denver. We'll settle into the neighborhood first. Then we'll get the kids going at school, and we'll slowly add extracurricular activities.

QUESTION 2

How specifically will I celebrate my successes along the way?

MY WORDS

How are you and your family going to celebrate your success in embracing this change?

RESPONSE

Once we're moved in, the whole family is going to take a three-day vacation in the mountains.

QUESTION 3

How will I keep moving toward my dreams, using all the resources this new beginning provides?

MY WORDS

Sue, one last thing. How are you going to keep moving toward your ultimate dreams, using your new resources?

RESPONSE

This move is just another step on our journey to the personal and financial goals Mike and I have set. We will use what we learn during this change to help us in our next transition!

In most trapeze acts, there is a person, called the "catcher," who hangs by the knees from the new bar and catches the person who is flying through the air as soon as she even gets close to the new bar. Life does the same thing. When you release the old bar and confidently and competently fly through the air—keeping your eyes open and focused on the new bar—life will reach out and catch you most of the time.

The good news is you don't have to be perfect! If you don't catch the new bar the first time, life will usually provide you with a safety net. If you do fall into the net, however, it's important to climb back up the ladder immediately and fly through the air again. This is exactly what trapeze artists do when they fall into the net. They know they must complete the maneuver they missed in order to regain their confidence.

Use what you learned from your first experiment to catch the new bar this time. Be flexible! Be persistent! Be focused! Be the kind of person who confidently catches the bar with a smile on your face!

Now, using our three Questions for Embracing the New, let's continue with the example of the same business change we used in Chapters 9 and 10.

Stage Three: Questions for Embracing The New In Your Business

QUESTION 1

What can we do first that will be easy to accomplish and help us to embrace the new?

MY WORDS

Mike, what are some easy successes your company can achieve immediately that will help everyone embrace the journey to the new?

RESPONSE

After we finish reorganizing and re-engineering at the company, we need to focus on two critical improvements to our products D and E. That's a small change, and one that we can get on the market immediately. We can also create a marketing plan to announce the product improvement in thirty days. And we can have a closeout sale of our old model—that will bring in some cash immediately!

QUESTION 2

How specifically will we celebrate our successes along the way?

MY WORDS

What are some ways your team and entire company can celebrate your successes along the way?

RESPONSE

When we bring out the improved products, we're going to have the most spectacular product/service unveiling we've ever had. Even before the unveiling, we'll have a huge appreciation party for our employees and their families. And if this re-engineering increases our profits like we think it will, we'll give a bonus to every single person in the company at the end of the year.

QUESTION 3

How will we keep moving toward our dreams, using all the resources this new beginning provides?

MY WORDS

How can you keep the vision of this new direction in front of the company on an ongoing basis? What resources is this new beginning providing that you can continue to use as you move forward?

RESPONSE

We'll continue to use the team approach to improve our products and services, as well as develop new ones. We'll actively solicit not only our customers' opinions, but also our employees'.

We will keep our focus on solving our customers' challenges by providing them with high-quality products and services. Our company will become a model of giving more value than our customers could ever expect. As a result, our market share and profitability should increase exponentially.

Congratulations! Your Reacting to Change journey is complete. You've let go of the old by answering the eight Stage One questions. You've transitioned between the old and the new by answering the seven Stage Two questions. And you've embraced the new by answering the three Stage Three questions. You've now mastered how to handle most changes that occur in your life in just three steps and eighteen questions!

Now it's time to apply the information you've learned in this chapter to a personal and a business change in your life. Turn the page and complete the following Exercises for Action.

THRIVING ON CHANGE

EXERCISES FOR ACTION

1. Using the same personal change that you
   selected in the Exercises for Action in the
   previous two chapters, develop a plan for Stage
   Three of Change Reaction, Embracing the
   New, by answering the three questions
   presented in this chapter and listed below. (P.S. Make sure
   you do the Mental Creation Exercise on page 215 first!)

   1. **What can I do first that will be easy to accomplish
      and help me to embrace the new?**

   2. **How specifically will I celebrate my successes
      along the way?**

   3. **How will I keep moving toward my dreams, using
      all the resources this new beginning provides?**

2. Using the same business change from the Exercises for
   Action in the previous two chapters, develop a plan for
   Embracing the New by answering the three questions
   presented in this chapter.

   1. **What can we do first that will be easy to
      accomplish and help us to embrace the new?**

   2. **How specifically will we celebrate our successes
      along the way?**

   3. **How will we keep moving toward our dreams, using
      all the resources this new beginning provides?**

In the last three chapters, you've learned how to respond to external change using the Three Stages of Change Reaction. You've become a daring and skilled trapeze artist! Now it's time to move ahead and learn the even more essential strategies of anticipating external change. The world is changing rapidly around you.

Read this chapter today and learn the power of . . .

Anticipating Change!

CHAPTER 12

Anticipating Change

Today, the winds of change are blowing from all directions. They're also stronger and more frequent than ever before. Is this good or bad? Well, it's bad for people and companies who aren't anticipating change, who aren't smart, quick, and flexible enough to maneuver their ships and set their sails appropriately. However, it's the opportunity of a lifetime for people and companies who correctly anticipate the winds of change and maneuver their ships and set their sails correctly.

James Clark and Marc Andreesen are two examples of being smart, flexible, and quick. They anticipated, far better than anyone (including Microsoft), a specific business trend: the explosive growth of the Internet. They created software that helps people cruise the

Internet and create Web sites. Their company, Netscape, is the fastest growing software company on record, with sales of $81 million in 1995 and expected sales of $230 million in 1996. When Netscape's initial public offering hit in 1995, the market valued the company's stock at $5 billion, making both Clark and Andreesen multi-million-aires in a day.

A football receiver also knows about anticipation. He runs to where the ball is going to be, not where it is at the time he first sees it in the air. Both personally and professionally, you need to run to where the ball is going to be on the playing field of your life!

Here are two additional examples of the power of anticipation:

- The man who designed the touch-tone phone put the "∗" and the "#" keys next to the zero on the keypad. Why? Because he anticipated that someday there might be a use for them. Boy, was he ever right!

- Bill Gates, the founder of Microsoft, knows the value of anticipation. In early 1994, when Microsoft was at the top of its industry with record earnings, Bill Gates announced a massive reorganization of the company. He knew the systems, processes, and strategies that had taken Microsoft to the top would not keep it there. He was smart enough to change before he had to.

Like Bill Gates, you, too, will need to master the art of anticipating change. The secret to successful change anticipation is the ability to look at the bigger picture. You need to be able to spot patterns of change: the directions in which your life, your business, and society as a whole is headed.

Patterns of Change

There are three significant patterns of change which you must be able to recognize:

- **Trends**

- **Progressions**

- **Cycles**

Later in this chapter, you will learn where to discover trends, progressions, cycles, as well as the questions you should ask to utilize these patterns of change to your advantage. You'll also see three real-world examples of change anticipation in action. First, let's define these three important patterns of change.

TRENDS

Trends are *definite, long-term (three years or more), and predictable directions in which a large segment of society is headed.* Trends are not fads. Fads are short-term (one- to three-year) changes in the behavior of a subgroup of our society. A fad may be teenagers wearing a particular style of clothing for a year. Most trends have (or will have) some degree of significance in your personal life and business.

To spot a trend, you need to identify changes in behavior in a society through time. If you notice a widespread change in group behavior at a certain point in time, then you see that behavior continuing and expanding over a period of years, you probably have spotted a trend. Sports-utility and four-wheel-drive vehicles are part of a trend you may have noticed over the last decade.

To spot patterns of change which are likely to become trends, you must first be observant of the changes in society around you, and then use your common sense to identify which of these changes are likely to grow into trends.

One example of a trend is "cocooning," which was first identified by Faith Popcorn in her book, *The Popcorn Report.* Cocooning occurs when people feel threatened by the external world;

therefore, they tend to stay in their safe, comfortable, controlled, and secure homes with their families. Here are just three examples of how cocooning affects what people do and the way they spend their money.

- Companies like Blockbuster Video—which provide home video and computer game rentals—are booming.

- Catalogs selling gardening tools and seeds are doing extremely well. In fact, mail order sales of all kinds have increased exponentially over the past few years. Why? You can shop the world without ever leaving home!

- Stores (like Boston Market) which specialize in take-out meals, and hot food delivery stores like Pizza Hut and Domino's Pizza are thriving.

The companies mentioned above have anticipated correctly the trend of cocooning, and they are prospering massively as a result.

Trends can often be spotted by looking for patterns in the following areas:

1. *Identify individuals, groups, and corporations who are achieving outstanding results in any field.* They may be the first to tap into a trend. Blockbuster Video and America Online are two examples of companies who were some of the first to tap into the trends of cocooning and online communication.

2. *Identify groups who are about to experience (or who are just beginning to experience) a significant amount of pain.* Others may soon feel the pain, which will provide the spark for a trend that moves the entire group.

   Netscape is an example of this. In the last five years the number of people who wanted to take advantage of the Internet grew by leaps and bounds, but most of them found it extremely difficult to navigate this vast, interconnected, uncharted universe. In other words, they were confused (in pain). Netscape's founders Clark and Andreessen saw the confusion and created a software product, Navigator, to ease it. Their superb pain detection coupled with decisive action has made them millionaires many times over.

3. *Identify groups about to experience (or just beginning to experience) a significant amount of pleasure.* Others may want to feel the pleasure, too, which will provide the spark for a trend that moves the group toward pleasure.

Nintendo owns a 40% share of the $15 billion electronic game market because it identified a group of people who were just beginning to experience a significant amount of pleasure. In the early 1980s they noticed a small but fiercely loyal group of teenagers popping quarters into video game machines in arcades around the world. So in 1985, Nintendo launched its first home video game console and created highly interactive games such as Donkey Kong to go with it. The result: In 1995 Nintendo sold its billionth game cartridge, and 141-millionth hardware system!

4. *Identify people who are intelligently and effectively questioning the status quo and doing things differently.* What these people are doing differently will be seen by others. If enough other people decide to do it, too, a trend will be created.

The Amway Corporation is definitely questioning the status quo and doing things differently. Their network marketing approach to the sales of products and services resulted in worldwide sales of $6.3 billion in 1995, up from $5.4 billion in 1994. Amway is on the front end of a huge trend that has plenty of room to grow.

PROGRESSIONS

The second pattern of change you will want to be able to identify is a progression. Like trends, progressions are directions; but while trends are directions in which society or a large segment of society is headed, progressions are *pathways that people, products, companies, etc., tend to take over the course of their lifetime.*

There are many different pathways people take through life. A common one is birth, early childhood before school, school-age childhood, teens, college and/or early working years, marriage, living without kids, living with kids, living without kids, retirement, and death. I'm currently in the married–living with kids stage of my life progression. I will be in it for another six years. My pathway is fairly straight for a while. But in five years, I'm going to have to anticipate and prepare for the curve in the road ahead when our youngest daughter, Belinda, leaves home to go to college or work.

Most consumer products go through a progression of introduction, growth, decline, and phase out. Smart businesses recognize this and either reconfigure their product before the end of the progression, or they introduce a new product to take the old product's place. Because of the fast pace of change in the computer industry, computer companies often introduce new products monthly to keep ahead of the progression.

Many companies also follow a progression of growth and decline over a period of years. Here's an example of a progression typical of many start-up companies today:

1. Company A is started by an innovative and dynamic entrepreneur.

2. Company A grows rapidly.

3. The entrepreneur who founded the company lacks the skills to run Company A at its new, expanded size.

4. Company A struggles to stay successful; entrepreneur is unhappy having to do things he or she doesn't enjoy.

5. Entrepreneur hires experienced CEO to run the new, larger Company A.

6. New CEO gets Company A back on track; entrepreneur starts another company!

No matter what progression you, your product, or your business are following, it's important to anticipate what the road ahead may have in store for you. If you don't, a sudden (yet predictable) turn in the road may cause you to lose control and crash. If you do anticipate the major turns on your pathway, you can make preparations ahead of time and joyfully navigate the turns with flair and grace!

CYCLES

The third pattern of change is a cycle. Cycles are *series of recurring events*. The winter-spring-summer-fall cycle is one example. You can see cycles clearly in the consumer products industry—certain products are going to be big sellers at Christmastime, but who's going to buy Christmas lights in July? If a retailer holds on to these holiday items until October and November, however, the lights will be flying off the shelves.

Fashion is nothing but cycles. How many times have you walked into a clothing store and thought to yourself, "I used to wear that style ten years ago! And now it's back!" Bellbottoms, platform shoes, wide flowery ties, and hemline lengths are all examples of fashion cycles in action.

Long-term investors in the stock market know the power of cycles. They know "what goes up, must come down," and vice versa. They utilize their knowledge of cycles to buy more shares when the market is down, knowing as long as the company is fundamentally sound, the stock price will rise again when the market rises.

In many ways, all our lives are cycles. There are times when everything is going great, then life throws us a curve ball and we get upset. The distress can be lessened by believing "This, too, shall pass"—and focusing on the fact that the cycle of life keeps rolling along!

When you encounter a particular change that feels somehow familiar, ask yourself, "Is this part of a recurring cycle? If so, what other changes can I anticipate will follow this particular stage in the cycle of change?"

Trends, progressions, and cycles are three different kinds of winds that occur on the sea of life. They are forces that come from different directions, at different times, in different intensities. Some are easily seen; others aren't. As the captain of your ship, you must anticipate correctly the most significant winds, prepare for their arrival, and point your ship in the proper direction by setting your sails at the appropriate angle. Failure to do so will slow the journey to your destination; or you could even capsize if the wind is strong enough. However, correct and timely anticipation of the winds, and proactive preparation of your ship will create a powerfully synergistic relationship between you and the winds of change. You will move rapidly past other ships toward your goals.

To stay one step ahead of life, you not only have to recognize patterns of change—you also have to utilize them. Here are the Three Change-Anticipation Steps that will help you use the winds of trends, progressions, and cycles to sail easily and eagerly ahead!

Three Change-Anticipation Steps

Step 1. Be knowledgeable.

Do your homework so you will have enough background information to spot the important trends, progressions, and cycles that are occurring in your personal life and business.

Step 2. Be alert and curious.

Ask the right questions so you can discover the answers you need to ride the winds of change.

Step 3. Be proactive.

Use your answers to take action now! Start moving your sails *before* the wind reaches you so you can successfully use the winds of change to sail ahead of your competition.

Step 1. Be knowledgeable.

The first thing I hear from people who have missed the boat by not anticipating change is, "I wish I'd known it was coming!" When it comes to change anticipation, what you don't know *can* hurt you. Being knowledgable is the first step in anticipating change.

To accurately spot patterns of change, you should be both an expert in your field and a student of general knowledge. Have a wide variety of friends. Get together with people outside your industry. A medical research assistant or graduate student in astronomy probably knew more about the Internet in 1992 than a computer programmer! Outsiders look at the world with fresh eyes. Tap into the power of their unique perspective.

Be knowledgeable about the happenings in your community, the nation, and the world. Get out there and actually talk to people, especially the ones who buy your products and services. Go to unusual places. That's where unusual ideas are found.

Here are some of the best places to identify and become knowledgable about trends, progressions, and cycles:

- At the minimum, read a major daily newspaper. Go deeper than the headlines—patterns of change are rarely major stories, especially in their infancy. Watch for the small items that pique your interest. For example, the Internet and the World Wide Web weren't well known outside of the military and the academic community for many years. Articles about this new way of connecting with other computers never appeared on the front page, but you could find a few references buried deep inside the computer or business section.

- Read *USA Today*. It's the best way I know to get concise information on hundreds of different topics. Just today, I read an article that described a poll indicating 70% of the Baby Boomers—the 76 million people born between 1946 and 1964—expect they will have second and even third careers after they officially retire. There will be tremendous training opportunities for these people. This is a trend I plan to take advantage of!

- Reputable, people-oriented magazines like *People*, *Newsweek*, and *Time* are excellent sources of trends, progressions, and cycles in general society.

- Business trends, progressions, and cycles can be discovered in magazines such as *Business Week*, *Forbes*, and *Fortune*, and newspapers such as *The Wall Street Journal*. Again, look for the little, curious stories deep in the paper or magazine.

- Newsletters in your area of interest are excellent sources of patterns of change that will impact you specifically.

- Keep your eyes and ears open to the world and all the people in it. Notice commonalties; listen for the "buzz."

- In your business, listen to the people who are closest to your customers. Your sales and customer service people are usually the ones who see changes the earliest. Actively elicit their suggestions, and get out there and serve your customers yourself. You'll see what's really going on.

One of the best ways to learn to use patterns of change to your advantage is to find people who are masters of the particular type of change you need to know about. Find someone who is an expert at tapping into product cycles, for example. Or perhaps you know someone who has taken a company through the startup–growth–going public–selling–moving on progression. Talk to a friend or acquaintance who has already experienced the change you're going through in your personal life—starting a second career, for example. Then use the modeling skills you learned in Chapter 6 to take advantage of their knowledge and mastery in the shortest possible time.

There are many excellent books available describing trends, progressions, and cycles in action. Read books such as Gail Sheehy's *New Passages*, Dan Burrus' *Technotrends*, Gerald Celente's *Trend Tracking*, Faith Popcorn's *The Popcorn Report* and *Clicking*, and John Naisbitt's *Megatrends*.

Using your knowledge as a base, you can now move on to Step Two of Change Anticipation.

Step 2. Be alert and curious. Ask the right questions.

Let me give you a graphic example of why it is important to be alert and curious. Read out loud the following sentence:

FINISHED FILES ARE THE RESULT
OF YEARS OF SCIENTIFIC STUDY
COMBINED WITH THE EXPERIENCE
OF MANY YEARS OF EXPERTS.

Now count the number of times the letter "F" appears in the sentence. Do not read any further until you have counted the Fs!

How did you do? I'll tell you: there are seven F's in the sentence. If you didn't see all seven F's, don't feel badly. About 90% of the thousands of people I work with each year don't see all the F's the first time they read it! Go back and find all seven F's now. If you still can't find them, read the sentence backward and pay special attention to the shortest word in the sentence.

Where did you probably miss one or more F's—possibly in the word *of*? Your eyes saw the F image in the word *of* on the paper, but the F image registered on your brain as a V. You've been conditioned through many years of reading to perceive inaccurately something that's right in front of your eyes!

Is it possible that there are other things right in front of your eyes which you don't see because you've been conditioned not to see them? You bet! You must be alert and curious in order to see these things. One of my goals in writing this book is to shake you up a little to get you to notice all the beneficial F's in your world!

The obscure we see eventually;

the completely obvious takes a little longer.

EDWARD R. MURROW

People who thrive on change take an expectant approach to life. They expect to find powerful ideas everywhere they go and in everything they do! When they read a book, magazine, or newspaper, they say to themselves, "There are one or more ideas here that I can use to improve my life and/or my business. It's up to me to discover them by being alert and curious." When they meet a rich person, they say to themselves, "This person has knowledge that can benefit me. I just have to ask the questions that will uncover these ideas."

Bring ideas in and entertain them royally,

for one of them may be the king!

MARK VAN DOREN

Remember, the first step of Change Anticipation is to be knowledgeable. In Step One, you identify the trends, progressions, and cycles in your world. The second step is to be alert and curious. That means asking the right questions! So, now that you're alert and curious here are some questions you will want to ask to get the most out of the trends, progressions, and cycles you identify or experience.

1. TRENDS

- "How mature is this trend right now?"
- "How could this trend affect me (my family, my company) in the days, weeks, months, and years ahead?" Brainstorm. Come up with as many ideas as possible. Then limit your ideas to the most probable.
- "What can I (my company) do to use this trend to my (our) advantage?"

2. PROGRESSIONS

- "What stage of this progression am I (is my product, my company) in right now?"
- "What could be the effect on me (my company, my product) in the days, weeks, months, and years ahead if this progression continues?"
- "How can I use this progression to my (our) advantage?"

3. CYCLES

- "Where am I (we, my company, our product) right now in the cycle?"

- "What might happen in the days, weeks, months, and years ahead if the cycle continues?"

- "How can I (we) use this cycle to my (our) advantage?"

You'll see examples of using all of these questions at the end of this chapter.

Using the information you discovered by being alert, curious, and asking the right questions, you can now move on to Step Three of Change Anticipation.

Step 3. Be proactive.
Use your answers and take action now!

Don't stop now—turn the information you discovered to your advantage by actually doing something. If you don't shift your sails to take advantage of the winds of change, you could capsize. Or someone else will use the information to their advantage and you will find yourself left in their wake, dead in the water.

Do the thing and you will have the power!

RALPH WALDO EMERSON

Here are two examples of anticipation in action. Back in 1992, Bill Clinton was nominated by the Democratic Party as its candidate for President. At first, Clinton's ideas didn't receive much attention because it didn't look like he was going to defeat incumbent George Bush in the general election. At convention time Clinton was way behind in the polls. But what happened as Clinton caught up with

Bush in the polls and eventually passed him? Clinton's ideas began to receive more attention.

Because I was knowledgeable (Step 1), and alert and curious (Step 2), I saw that Clinton's promise to drastically revise the way health care is delivered in the U.S. was attracting a lot of attention from those in the health care delivery system. I could see that they were beginning to experience a fair amount of pain. I got creative and asked myself the right question: "What services can I offer health care providers to decrease their pain?" So I created a series of training programs called *Change, Challenge, and Choice: The Art of Thriving in Our Rapidly Changing Health Care Environment.* I then took immediate action (Step 3): I contacted a wide variety of health care associations and corporations about these trainings. The results have been fantastic!

The Levi Strauss Company perpetually anticipates change in their design decisions. The Baby Boomers had been a large part of the market for Levis ever since the '60s, and they weren't about to give up wearing jeans just because they were getting older! However, as the years passed Boomers were putting on a few pounds in inconvenient places. So Levi Strauss helped the Boomers get out of the pain of tight jeans by producing a line of "relaxed fit" (the politically correct way to say more room in the rear and thighs) jeans. You need to be the Levi Strauss of your product, service, or life. You must anticipate the trends that will eventually affect you.

The following are examples of how you can use the Change Anticipation Steps in a personal setting, in a business setting, and with a product. My friends Henry and Catherine were getting ready for a major milestone in their life progression: Their youngest child, Tom, was graduating from high school and going away to college in about a month. Henry and Catherine were going to be alone in the house for the first time in twenty-eight years. They used the Change Anticipation Steps to help them prepare for this transition.

Three Change Anticipation Steps for
a Progression in Your Personal Life

STEP 1. BE KNOWLEDGEABLE.

MY WORDS

Henry and Catherine, what knowledge would be helpful in managing the changes you believe you'll encounter as a part of this progression?

RESPONSE

First, we're going to read a book on the "empty nest" syndrome. Then we're going to talk to our friends Jim and Nancy about how they handled it. Their marriage seems better as a result of their last child leaving home. And we're going to talk to each other about how we feel and what we'd like to see happen in our relationship as we move into this new stage.

STEP 2. BE ALERT AND CURIOUS.

Ask the Right Questions.

....

MY WORDS

What stage of this progression are you in right now?

RESPONSE

We've been through the "dating–getting married–having children–raising children" phases of our relationship. We're about to move into the "living without children" phase.

MY WORDS

What could be the effect on you in the days, weeks, months, and years ahead if this progression continues?

RESPONSE

It will be a pretty big change—after all, we've had at least one child in our home for the last twenty-eight years. As we see it, there are three ways this could affect us.

One, our marriage could be weaker with Tom gone. I've seen this happen to other "empty nesters." For the last twenty-eight years, a lot of our time was spent being involved with the kids and their activities. We really don't want to see that happen—after all, we were together before we ever had kids, and we'd like to think our relationship has grown richer over the years. We're more interesting people, too!

Two, our marriage could proceed as it has been, which is busy and very good. That would be okay, but we'd rather use this as an opportunity for growth in our relationship with each other.

Three, our marriage could be enhanced with our last child out of the house. We will still be involved with Tom at college, as well as our older daughter, who's married with kids of her own now. Tom's the kind of kid who will bring home friends regularly, so we won't be losing touch with him, but now we'll have more time to travel together.

There are a lot of things we've always wanted to do, but never had the time to really explore. We've been thinking of joining a tennis club and playing mixed-doubles. And Catherine's been asked to run for a seat on the school board.

MY WORDS

How can you use this progression to your advantage?

RESPONSE

We're going to choose to make our marriage better! We're going to follow most of the advice that Jim and Nancy gave us. We'll take the trips to New England and Mexico we've been thinking about, and we'll stop off to see our daughter on the way home. When we get back, we're going to join the tennis club, and Catherine will see about the school board candidacy. We'll go up to see Tom at school a couple of times a year, and we've told him that he and his college friends are welcome in our home any time.

STEP 3. BE PROACTIVE.

Use Your Answers and Take Action Now!

· ·

MY WORDS

What actions can we take right now to anticipate this change?

RESPONSE

We'll get started on our plan today. Catherine, you call the tennis club and I'll call our travel agent. And let's set aside one night a week for a "date night" so we can get used to being just us two again. I'll bet we'll enjoy that a lot!

As an example of how to use the Three Change-Anticipation Steps with a particular trend, let's take a look at how Packard Bell anticipated and utilized the explosive growth of the home computer marketplace.

Three Change Anticipation Steps for a Business Trend

STEP 1. BE KNOWLEDGEABLE.

QUESTION

What knowledge would be helpful in managing the changes you believe you'll encounter as a part of this trend?

RESPONSE

In the late 1980s, Packard Bell saw that a small but ever-increasing number of people who used personal computers at work were also beginning to use them at home. They also saw a trend in parents buying computers for their children to use.

Packard Bell saw that only Apple Computer seemed to be going after the home computer market, and that Apple's machines were priced much higher than IBM-compatible PCs. They also noticed that most personal computers were sold primarily in specialized computer stores that intimidated the average home computer buyer.

STEP 2. BE ALERT AND CURIOUS.

Ask the Right Questions.

....

QUESTION

How mature is this trend right now?

RESPONSE

Packard Bell discovered the home PC trend was definitely in its infancy.

QUESTION

How could this trend affect our company in the days, weeks, months, and years ahead?

RESPONSE

The people at Packard Bell said, "If we can produce a line of reasonably priced PCs and sell them in stores that consumers are used to shopping in (like Sears, Wal-Mart, Circuit City, etc.), we can outflank IBM, Apple, and Compaq, because none of them are aggressively pursuing the home PC market in this way."

QUESTION

What can our company do to use this trend to its advantage?

RESPONSE

Cost was a very important consideration for home PC buyers. Packard Bell used outsourcing and the latest technology to produce a line of reasonably priced and technologically advanced PCs. They created several ready-to-use computer systems that sold for under $2,000.

They also established extremely close relationships with retailers like Sears, Wal-Mart, Staples, Circuit City, and Best Buy. Packard Bell observed, "We can show these retailers how to do a better job of marketing and selling computers. They're not doing a very good job of it now!"

STEP 3. BE PROACTIVE.

Use Your Answers and Take Action Now!

. . . .

QUESTION

What actions can our company take right now to anticipate this change?

RESPONSE

Packard Bell created a line of attractively priced home computer systems that were, in many cases, technologically advanced. They were the first company to deliver PCs with the operating system and key software applications already installed. This saved the consumer hassle and expense. Packard Bell was also the first to offer a toll-free support line, to include an internal CD-ROM drive, and to offer home computer users machines powered by Intel's Pentium® chips.

Packard Bell then formed close relationships with key retailers by becoming their partners in the computer business. They created in-store displays and demonstrations and trained the retailer's salespeople. It gave its retailers co-op advertising money to spend in local publications. Packard Bell has done its partnership job so well that it has won Vendor of the Year awards from Sears, Wal-Mart, and Staples!

Packard Bell is an excellent example of anticipating a trend with a particular kind of product and benefiting massively as a result. Now let's take a look at another example of anticipating a cycle in business—an example I have personal experience with.

Three Change-Anticipation Steps for a Business Cycle

STEP 1. BE KNOWLEDGEABLE.

QUESTION

What knowledge would be helpful in managing the changes we believe we'll encounter as a part of this cycle?

RESPONSE

For the past five or six years, I've noticed that more and more people I speak with on my travels around the U.S. are pessimistic about the future. Believing this shift toward pessimism was part of a cyclical shift of our national mood (which goes up and down with regularity), I started doing some research. Two *Business Week*/Harris polls confirmed my thinking. People were asked, "Compared to your life now, do you expect that your children will have a better life, a worse life, or a life about as good?"

In August 1988, the results were:

59% Better • **25% About as good** • **10% Worse**

By February 1996, however, the results were:

50% Better • **26% About as good** • **16% Worse**

That's a nine-point drop in people's confidence level! That information, coupled with all the publicity about societal ills, corporate downsizing and job insecurity, deterioration of our nation's "moral fiber," added to my own personal informal surveys and observations, made me believe we were definitely on the pessimistic side of the cycle of our national mood.

STEP 2. BE ALERT AND CURIOUS.

Ask the Right Questions.

QUESTION

Where are we as a nation right now in this cycle?

RESPONSE

When I first began asking this question (in the early '90s), I believed we were still early in the pessimism downswing.

QUESTION

What might happen in the days, weeks, months, and years ahead if the cycle continues?

RESPONSE

First, I thought if this cycle continues its downswing, my friends, my family, and maybe even me, Joe Optimistic, could begin to fall into pessimism. That would never do!

Second, I thought this pervasive pessimism might significantly affect my customers at corporations and associations. They might not want to do as much training as they had in the past, and they might not hire me. That really made me pessimistic!

Luckily, I came up with a third, more optimistic alternative. I thought, what if this cycle could actually benefit me? What if companies and associations saw how pessimistic their people were becoming, and as a result want to bring in someone (me) who could install optimism in its place? Wouldn't they feel an even greater need to give their people powerful tools to use change to everyone's advantage—tools I'm perfectly positioned to provide?

QUESTION

How can I use this cycle to my advantage?

RESPONSE

Here are the solutions I came up with:

- I began to collect statistics like, "In the U.S. between 1987 and 1991, Fortune 500 companies reduced their number of employees by 2.4 million. In that same time span, companies of twenty or fewer employees added a total of 4.4 million workers." You always see headlines like, "AT&T lays off 40,000!" You rarely see, "Mary's Software hires three computer programmers." I collected these statistics because I didn't feel the downswing of pessimism had much basis in fact. I wanted proof to back up my assumptions.

- I began to share my feelings of optimism and thoughts on the subject of change utilization with my friends and family. I saw it helped them to stand fast in the face of the pessimism they encountered in others.

- I took the materials I had collected and created a training program called "Thriving on Change" (the basis of this book).

STEP 3. BE PROACTIVE.

Use Your Answers and Take Action Now!

QUESTION

What actions can I take right now to anticipate this cycle?

RESPONSE

I immediately started marketing my new program to my corporate and association clients. Today, 60% of my business comes from training programs that help people overcome pessimism and use change to their advantage.

There are thousands of trends, progressions, and cycles operating in your world right now that you can use to your advantage. The question is, are you going to

Step 1. Be knowledgeable,
Step 2. Be alert and curious—ask the right questions, and
Step 3. Be proactive—use your answers to take action now?

. . . or are you going to remain ignorant about these trends, progressions, and cycles—and pay the price of missed opportunities? The choice is yours!

Remember learning about the power of mental focus in Chapter 8? You have the ability to travel through time by focusing on the past, present, or the future. Anticipation is focusing on the future in a way that will enable you to utilize change to create the life you desire and deserve. The *best time* to think about your future is now!

THE BEST TIME

The best time to think about retiring
is when you're twenty.

♦

The best time to acquire new job skills
is before you need them.

♦

The best time to give your kids quality time
is before there are challenges.

♦

The best time to "work on" your marriage
is before you need to.

♦

The best time to treat our planet right
is before it's too late.

♦

The best time to create your future is now!

NATE BOOTH

Let's apply the information in this chapter to anticipating the changes in your life by completing the Exercises for Action beginning on the next page.

EXERCISES FOR ACTION

1. Identify one personal change that may impact
    you in the days, weeks, months, or years ahead.
    Will there be a change in the make-up of your
    family? Will your children be leaving home?
    Are you getting a personal computer and going online?
    Would you like to start a fitness training program? Go back
    to school? Take a position of responsibility in your church
    or community? In your journal, write the change you will
    be experiencing in the future.

    Now, using the Three Change-Anticipation Steps, develop
    a plan to utilize this change to your advantage.

    STEP 1. Be knowledgeable. Do your homework.

    How would you identify this change? Is it a

    *   trend (a change that you are experiencing as part of a
        large segment of society—getting a personal computer,
        for example)

    *   progression (part of the pathway you are taking
        through life—having a child, or retiring)

    *   cycle (a recurring event—e.g., you assume leadership of
        your church's fundraising campaign every three years,
        or you go on a family vacation every year)

    What knowledge would be helpful in managing the
    changes you believe you'll encounter as part of this change?

STEP 2. Be alert and curious. Ask the right questions.

What stage of the change are you in right now? Or when do you anticipate this change will begin?

What could be the positive and negative effects on your life when this change occurs?

How can you use this change to your advantage?

STEP 3. Be proactive.
Use your answers and take action now!

What actions can you take right now to anticipate this change successfully?

2. Identify one change that may impact your business or profession in the days, weeks, months, or years ahead. In your journal, write the change your business will be experiencing in the future.

   Now, using the Three Change-Anticipation Steps, develop a plan to utilize this change to your business's advantage.

STEP 1. Be knowledgeable. Do your homework.

How would you identify this change? Is it a

- trend (a change that your business is experiencing as part of a larger segment of society)

- progression (part of the pathway your business is taking)

- cycle (a recurring event)

What knowledge would be helpful in managing the changes you believe your business will encounter as part of this change (progression, trend, cycle)?

STEP 2. Be alert and curious. Ask the right questions.

What stage of the change (progression, trend, cycle) is your business in right now, or when do you anticipate this change will begin?

What could be the positive and negative effects on your business when this change occurs?

How can your business use this change to its advantage?

STEP 3. Be proactive.
Use your answers and take action now!

What actions can your business take right now to anticipate this change successfully?

In the real world, sometimes you need to react to change. As much as possible, you also need to anticipate external change and make proactive internal changes. At other times, you will want to create change and be a leader. To learn how, read the next chapter.

Become a master at . . .

Creating Change!

CHAPTER 13

Creating Change

I believe that thriving on change can be summed up with a revision of a familiar prayer:

> *"God grant me the flexibility to react to change,*
>
> *the foresight and clarity to anticipate change,*
>
> *the courage to create change when needed,*
>
> *and the wisdom to know when to do each!"*

In this chapter, you will learn how to create change when it is needed. Effective change creators ride the waves of their own creation, and other people react to their waves!

First, you will learn how to create change in your personal life, and then how to create it in your business life. In both cases, there is a series of simple steps you can use to create your wave of change.

Six Steps for Creating Change in Your Personal Life

Step 1. Go on an unquestioned conviction hunt.

An unquestioned conviction is *a rigid and persistent belief that a person or group holds and has never challenged.* Your unique collection of unquestioned convictions provides a degree of security because it keeps out all other beliefs and creates order in your world. You have the security of believing totally, "This is the way it is!" However, unquestioned convictions can also put a wall around your thinking and suppress innovative ideas. You probably have unquestioned convictions that were formed at some point in your life. Those convictions may have supported you then—but they may be limiting you now.

Recently I spoke with a friend who had an unquestioned conviction that his present job wasn't preparing him for what he truly wanted to do. As a result, he felt bored and out of place at work. He didn't approach his present job with any passion or sense of purpose. As you might imagine, this attitude was slowing his progress toward his dream job! When I got my friend to challenge his unquestioned conviction by showing him several ways his present job would be superb training for the job he really wanted, his entire attitude changed. His results improved dramatically, and he was able to leave this company a year later to take the job he'd always dreamed of.

There are unquestioned convictions lurking around almost every corner in business. For example, throughout most of the twentieth century the U.S. railroad companies had an unquestioned conviction that they were in the railroad business. If they had challenged that conviction early on and realized that they were in the *transportation* business instead, they would probably be a more dominant force in passenger travel in the U.S.—the way railroads are in Europe and Japan, where high-speed trains carry thousands of passengers each day.

Unquestioned convictions in a company are taught to new employees by the old guard—those who "know how things really work around here." The absence of unquestioned convictions is often why people new to a company can come up with fantastically original ideas the first month on the job. They haven't learned the boundaries that limit the old pros!

If you want to know about water, don't ask a fish.

MARSHALL MCLUHAN

You want to be one of the new guard, not the old pros. In business and in life, seek out unquestioned convictions. Question what, where, when, how, with whom, and why you do something. Question every-thing—*except* universal principles, and the relationships and habits they foster.

Just because you question something doesn't mean that you're dissatisfied with it or are necessarily going to change it. Just think of it as looking at your life with fresh eyes. Remember the curiosity of a five-year-old child and ask yourself what, where, when, who, how, and why about almost everything.

Here are some questions you can use to get your unquestioned conviction hunt off to a great start.

1. What parts of your day do you least enjoy?

2. What parts of your day are just busy work?

3. What ideas, procedures, and habits seem outdated?

4. What ideas, procedures, and habits have you inherited from a parent, friend, or predecessor?

5. If the comic strip character Dilbert or your favorite stand-up comic were to make fun of your life, what parts would give them the best material?

In the 1960s, the high-jumper Dick Fosbury went on an unquestioned conviction hunt. The universally accepted approach used by all his competitors was the "Western Roll," where the high-jumper approached the bar at a 30-degree angle and went over the bar, stomach toward the ground, with one arm leading the way. Fosbury questioned everything about that approach, and as a result he created "The Fosbury Flop." He approached the bar at a 45- to 60-degree angle and went over the bar with his back to the ground and his head leading the way. Dick Fosbury won the gold medal in the 1968 Olympics with this new approach. The Fosbury Flop is still the method of choice in high-jumping today—just waiting for another "Fosbury" to question it and take the sport to the next level.

Let me show you how I recently helped another friend create positive change in his life by examining one of his unquestioned convictions about his kids. Paul's son Barry was about to graduate from high school, and instead of going directly to college, he wanted to join the armed services. As a CPA who had gotten straight A's and gone from high school to college to graduate school before entering the business world, Paul was very upset about his son's career choice.

Paul's unquestioned conviction was, "You've got to go to college and get advanced degrees to open the doors to the highest levels of success."

I asked Paul the following *what, where, when, who, how,* and *why* questions about his conviction. Here are his answers.

QUESTION

Paul, what *actions does this belief cause you to take or not to take?*

RESPONSE

Well, I've spent the last two years of Barry's time in high school researching colleges for him, talking to him about the career paths he might want to take. The first time he told me he was interested in the military, I exploded. We had a huge fight and I didn't feel comfortable around him for at least a week. I told him he would have to wait until he was eighteen to enlist, because I wasn't going to sign the papers for him. I also deliberately missed some of the activities associated with his graduating from high school because I was so upset.

QUESTION

Where is this belief affecting your life negatively?

RESPONSE

It's pretty obvious that it's had a terrible affect on my relationship with my son. This was going to be such a special time for us—he's the oldest of our children, and I was really looking forward to seeing him graduate and sending him off to college in the fall. I was even secretly hoping he might go to my alma mater, and now that's gone. Mostly, I'm worried about Barry, about his future. I can't see how anyone can take four or more years before they go to college and not spend their whole lives catching up with the people who went directly from high school.

This whole thing is also affecting my relationship with Keesha, my wife. Once Barry made his decision she really supported him, and even though we've talked about it, I feel pretty isolated because she's on his side. And I'm feeling ashamed around my friends at work.

How can I tell them my son, one of the brightest kids in his class, the kid I've been bragging about for so many years, is not going to college but is joining the military?

QUESTION

When *does this belief hinder you?*

RESPONSE

All the time. With my family. With my kids. With my colleagues. With myself. I don't like myself much right now because of the way I feel. And I don't see how I can change the way I feel while Barry's in the military, unless I change this belief.

QUESTION

Paul, with whom *are you connected as a result of this belief? Does this belief truly support the relationship, or does it cause separation?*

RESPONSE

This belief causes nothing but separation. It's especially evident because this is a time where I should be most connected with the people I care about—Barry, Keesha, the rest of my family and friends.

QUESTION

How *does this belief possibly hold you back from creating changes that will benefit you?*

RESPONSE

Unless I come up with a different way of looking at the situation or something else to believe, I run the risk of permanently alienating my son. It's unlikely he'll ever listen to my guidance again, and more important, we'll never have the same kind of close relationship we've shared through the years. To be quite honest, this belief has also held me back from respecting the talents and choices of a lot of people I've encountered through the years who never went to college but succeeded anyway. I can see now I have a tendency to look down on those people because they weren't as "educated" as I was. Perhaps their education just came from different sources—experience, or other people. Even though I'm proud of my education and how hard I had to work to get the grades, maybe I need to recognize the accomplishments of others as equal or even better than my own.

QUESTION

Paul, with all this information available to you about the negative consequences of this old belief, why not change now?

RESPONSE

Yes—why not? This belief certainly isn't doing me any good, and changing it can eliminate a lot of pain and create new ways of relating to my son and others.

QUESTION

So, what will your new belief be?

RESPONSE

My new belief is that education can come from many places, and people can create their own opportunities—especially if they're allowed to choose their own paths.

QUESTION

And what will be the positive consequences of your new belief?

RESPONSE

I'll feel very differently about Barry's choice of the military. I know he's a great kid, and I have complete confidence in his abilities. The first thing I'll do is have a talk with him, tell him I was wrong, and give him my complete support. I'll tell him how proud I am of him, and how sure I am that no matter what he chooses to do, he'll be great at it because of who he is.

Then I'll talk to Keesha and the rest of the kids. I owe them an apology, too—I've been impossible to live with for the last few months. This new belief will really affect the way I relate to all of them. Each of the kids is so different, and I've been expecting them to fit into the "get good grades so you can go to a good college" mold. While I still want them to do well, I'm going to be a lot more open to recognizing their strengths in every area, not just school. After all, "people smarts" and teamwork are important, too!

When I go into work tomorrow, I'm going to brag about Barry. After all, it takes guts to make a decision to become a man at eighteen, instead of staying in school and depending on his family financially for another four years. It'll be great to talk to my colleagues again about my kids. And you know what? There's a young woman in my department who's up for a promotion. She's been doing great work for the last two years, but she doesn't have her advanced accounting degree so I wasn't seriously considering her. I'm going to spend some time with her, talk to her supervisor more, and if I think she has the ability I'll promote her whether she has the degree or not.

Remember, beliefs are the foundation upon which we build our lives, but they can also keep us from the changes we want and need. So take inventory of your unquestioned convictions—and, like Dick Fosbury, you may revolutionize your life as a result!

Step 2. Be alert for innovative ideas everywhere.

Be on a constant lookout for innovative ideas from all walks of life. One of the best ways to do this is to vary your routine. Don't read the same newspapers and magazines, listen to the same music, watch the same television programs, go to the same restaurants, or do the same things on weekends. Don't hang out with same people all the time. In fact, cultivate a few friends that are genuine "wackos"! Regularly ask yourself these questions: "Who thinks differently than I do? And what have I learned from them today?" Most people ask the opposite—they say, "Who thinks like I do, and how can they reinforce my present thinking?"

Put some variety in your life! It will put you face to face with innovative ideas you've never seen before. If you expand your world, you'll be more likely to discover unconventional ideas, and then you can use them to create change in your life.

To become more alert to innovative ideas all around you, in your journal list three ways you're committed to adding variety to your life, whether it be reading something new, taking up a new hobby or sport, visiting a new restaurant, or learning a new skill. Next to each, give yourself a deadline to start this new activity, and make sure it is within the next two weeks.

Step 3. Break the pattern of thinking in a linear fashion.

When you think in a linear fashion, you're thinking that events will be connected in a straight line, from the past through the present to the future. Even in our rapidly changing world, linear thinking is appropriate at certain times—but straight-line thinking won't lead you very well when the road takes an unexpected turning! The Encyclopedia Britannica people went out of business because they stuck to their linear thinking that print encyclopedias would always be needed, instead of recognizing the "turn in the road" represented by CD-ROM technology.

The results of outdated linear thinking are all around us. The thirteen-week summer vacation most schools still use was originally created so children could help their parents tend the crops in the field. That was appropriate thinking in the 1800s when 98% of the population lived on farms. Now that less than 2% of us live on farms, maybe it's time we stopped thinking linearly and devised an accelerated schedule for our students.

Instead of thinking linearly all the time, you need to think in *cyclical*, *parallel*, and *discontinuous* fashions. With *cyclical* thinking, you think in cycles, not a straight line. The four seasons (winter, spring, summer, fall) metaphor I used earlier is an example of cyclical thinking. My wife Dawn knows about cycles when it comes to fashion. She buys well-made clothing, wears it for a couple of years, puts it in storage when it's out of style, and then wears it again when it's back in style twenty years later!

The U.S.–Soviet Union arms race was a series of events that should have been viewed cyclically. The cycle we should have seen was

If the U.S. and/or the Soviet Union would have viewed the arms race as a true cycle, either one could have broken the cycle at any point.

With *parallel* thinking, two or more processes are occurring and progressing at the same time. For example, when your daughter gets married, it's not an ending of the relationship with your daughter— it's the beginning of a parallel relationship between two separate and related families.

Parallel thinking allows countries to embrace cultural diversity. The people of a minority culture can keep their culture alive and still be part of the overall culture of a nation.

With *discontinuous* thinking, you realize that processes stop and start in a seemingly haphazard fashion. There is no smooth flow. As an important example, just because you've lived with and depended upon your spouse for thirty years doesn't mean that person is going to be around for the rest of your life. Hard as it may be to think about, you need to make financial plans now to prepare for the possibility of your or your spouse's premature death.

As you can see, linear thinking can only get you so far. By utilizing the skills of cyclical, parallel, and discontinuous thinking, you can see the events of your life in an entirely new way, opening up to greater possibilities. It's time to "get out of line" and think in new ways!

Step 4. Ask questions you've never asked before, and then answer the questions creatively.

To receive answers you've never gotten before, ask questions you've never asked before. Three powerful questions you can ask are the personal innovation questions you learned in Chapter 6.

1) What if I could _____?

2) What if I didn't have to _____?

3) What if I could _____ *and* _____?

You can also ask these two questions:

4) What one change (if it did happen) would revolutionize my life?

5) What one or two changes in my life would move me closer to my dream?

A couple of weeks ago, I was speaking with a friend who was stuck. I could see she needed some new and empowering answers in her life. So I had two choices: 1) *Tell* her what I thought she should do, or 2) *ask* her questions that would assist her to come up with her own best answer.

By now, you should know the choice I made. I said, "Mary, I know it seems like you're a little stuck in your life right now, but what one change, if it did happen, would revolutionize your life?" The question apparently opened the right file in her mind, because she went on for about ten minutes with a list of all the changes that would improve her life. I listened carefully and then asked, "Of all the things you just came up with, which ones could you get started on today?" She came up with three specific actions she could take. Because I know that there is a huge difference between "could-ing" and "committing," I asked, "Are you just talking, or are you committed to doing these three things today?" She replied, "I'm committed to doing them!"

I said, "Great! Give me a call at 9 P.M. to let me know how you're doing." With a big smile on her face, she said, "Sure!"

In this case, I asked the questions for my friend. You don't have the luxury of having a friend constantly at your side, but you *can* become a master at asking your own creative questions. What will happen in your life when you learn to do this now?

Step 5. Create a "why" list to inspire action.

Create a huge list of the "whys"—the reasons behind your making the change now. If you have enough "whys" in your life, you'll figure out how.

Here's an example of a "why" list that inspired me to act. For a long time, I'd wanted to stop going to the office so much. I wanted to hire an assistant to do all the "busy" work at the office. Then I could work at home on all the creative things that I enjoy. As you probably know from your own life, "wanting" is usually not enough to get you to take action! So I created the following "why" list:

1. I won't have to do all that office stuff I don't enjoy.

2. I can do more of the creative things I really love.

3. I'll be able to finally write that book I've been talking about for a year.

4. I'll be able to spend more time with my wife and daughter.

5. I won't have to spend an hour each day on the highway.

6. Now I can justify buying all that neat, new home office equipment.

7. I'll have more flexibility in my life. If I want to go hit golf balls for an hour, I can.

Doing my "why" list pushed me over the edge. I convinced the "suits" at my company to allow Penny Morris, my wonderful new partner, to work with me 30 hours a week. I went out and bought all the neat new home office technology machines I could stuff in my car trunk. I had a zillion new telephone lines brought into my home to handle all the information pouring in and out of the office. Now I'm a happy man, sitting here typing this book!

Step 6. Just do it!

Remember—the Nike people are right!

You miss 100% of the shots you never take.

WAYNE GRETZKY

These same six steps can be used in business to create the levels of change needed to keep up in a very competitive world. Businesses today have to create a "Fosbury Flop" almost every year, because staying where you are actually means falling farther and farther behind. Use the following five steps with your business, and you can ride the resulting waves of change to greater profits and greater success!

Five Steps to Creating Change in Your Business

Step 1. Go on an unquestioned conviction hunt.

Challenge every aspect of your company's current thinking, beliefs, systems, processes, products, and services. Over and over ask the question, "What if there were a better way?" Be on the lookout for phrases like, "That's impossible!" or "We've never done things like that around here!" or "I wish it were that easy!"—especially if it comes from an "expert" who has been around a while!

Experts can have the most difficulty when it comes to change in their area of expertise, for then they would have to admit they were wrong or outdated. Cast a wary eye toward the expert holding on to the old despite the light of the new!

Company policy means that there's no

understandable reason for this action.

HERBERT PROCHNOW

The CEO of Taco Bell, John Martin, isn't afraid to make changes. In 1982, Taco Bell was a $500 million regional company. By 1992, in a stagnant fast food industry, Taco Bell was a $3 billion international company! The advice from its ads, "Run for the border!" is heeded by hundreds of thousands of people each day. John says that Taco Bell is successful "because we listen to our customers and are not afraid to change."

Reinvention, as described in Chapter 6, is taking your corporate unquestioned conviction hunt to its height.

Step 2. Be alert for innovative ideas everywhere.

Look everywhere for ideas. Robert Weisman got the idea for "billboards" in public bathrooms when he sat in a bathroom stall, staring at the back of a stall door. He parlayed that idea into a $12-million-a-year company, Stallwords.

Jim Jenks got the idea for Ocean Pacific sportswear by looking down at a restaurant tablecloth and thinking, "This would make a great pair of swim trunks!" He then took action and created "jams" and "baggies" which are perfect both for surfing and eating pizza.

Over 90% of business people use Post-it Notes. The glue used on Post-its was originally thought to be a failure because it held so poorly. Luckily for 3M, one of its chemists, Arthur Fry, didn't think that way. He thought it would make an effective glue for holding notes in his hymnal at church!

In his fantastic book, *If It Ain't Broke . . . BREAK IT!*, Robert Kriegel asks,

Question: What do the following all have in common?
Cornflakes. The microwave. Post-its. Walkman®. Teflon®.
Scotchgard™. Aspartame. Vulcanized rubber. Rogaine. Kitty
litter. Ivory® soap. Velcro®. Rayon. Frozen food. Skateboards.

Answer: None of these common, now seemingly indispensable
products was planned. They were all accidents, unexpected
treasures found by observant individuals paying attention to
something that was right in front of their noses. The man
who created Velcro discovered the idea as he was pulling
burrs out of his socks!

Johnson & Johnson got into the baby powder business by
accident. In the late 1800s, J&J was a major supplier of antiseptic
gauze and medical plasters for casts. A few doctors complained about
irritation on the skin of some of their patients, so J&J began including
a small can of Italian talcum powder with their gauze and plaster
products. To their surprise, their customers began asking for more
talc than gauze and plaster! J&J Baby Powder eventually grew to be
44% of its business.

In 1920, a J&J employee created a small ready-to-use bandage for
his wife who had the habit of cutting herself with knives. Lucky for J&J
that she was a little clumsy, or they may have never marketed Band-Aids®!

You never know where or when the idea will strike you. Be
alert for innovative ideas everywhere.

Step 3. Break the pattern of thinking in a linear fashion.

Again, when you think in linear fashion, you think that today
is pretty much like yesterday and tomorrow will be pretty much like
today. Maybe linear thinking worked in the '50s, but it certainly
doesn't work in most rapidly changing business situations. Linear
thinking assumes the status quo will remain constant, which is a
dangerous thing to do these days. When was the last time you bought
a vinyl record or had your carburetor tuned up?

In fact, past successes can be your worst enemy. Past successes can lead to linear thinking, because you believe that the same strategies that produced success in the past will produce the same kind of success in the future. This is a dangerous assumption in times of rapid change.

Bill Gates isn't making that assumption. He isn't thinking in a linear fashion with his reorganization of Microsoft. He is not making predictions of tomorrow based on the assumptions of today. In fact, he's assuming tomorrow will be drastically different!

In business, it's vital that you begin to think in cyclical, parallel, and discontinuous fashions. Here are a few examples of each.

1. Cyclical thinking

In his book, *Unlimited Wealth*, Paul Pilzer reveals there are predictable cycles of optimism and pessimism in our economy. Harry Dent's, *The Great Boom Ahead* has numerous graphs illustrating the predictable cycles of growth and recession. Look for and study thinkers who are aware of the big picture and can see cycles developing over time.

2. Parallel thinking

Steven Nichols knows the power of parallel thinking. In 1986 he bought a small athletic shoe company called K-Swiss. He knew K-Swiss couldn't compete against giants like Nike and Reebok—those companies poured considerable resources into hundreds of different models and styles of athletic shoes in order to capture the fickle teenage market. The average lifetime of each Nike or Reebok model is only four months!

So K-Swiss took a *parallel* approach. It made shoes for the more mature market of serious sports enthusiasts, weekend athletes, and tennis players. K-Swiss's only model was called the Classic. As the name implies, the Classic is designed to be on the market for years. Steven Nichols' parallel strategy is working. K-Swiss has gone from $20 million in sales in 1986 to $150 million in 1993!

Snapple did the same thing in the fiercely competitive soft drink market. For years Snapple owned the bottled tea segment because of its unique parallel marketing strategy. They didn't compete with Coke and Pepsi head on—that would have been disaster. Snapple took the "natural" route, claiming their products were made from "the best stuff on earth!"

Snapple didn't spend millions on slick advertising campaigns. Instead, it advertised on Howard Stern's radio show and got its products in the hands of Howard's loyal fans almost overnight. Snapple went from a few thousand cases sold in 1986 to 25 million cases in 1992!

In his book, *Megatrends*, John Naisbitt gives another example of parallel thinking. The megatrend of "high tech" and "high touch" developed together. The coldness of high tech in our lives is counterbalanced by the warm fuzzy of high touch. Both of these trends are needed in the '90s. You can hop between them with parallel thinking.

3. Discontinuous thinking

The Swiss watch industry got caught in the trap of linear thinking when it should have been thinking discontinuously. In 1968 the Swiss had 65% of the worldwide sales of watches and more than 80% of the profits. They had been the leader in watch manufacturing and technology ever since the watch was invented. Unfortunately for them, their past success was their worst enemy.

In 1967, the Swiss themselves developed the quartz movement for watches. But because they were linear thinkers, they believed the quartz movement would never rival their time-tested mechanical movement. The Japanese company Seiko thought differently. It used discontinuous thinking and created high quality quartz watches at drastically lower prices. By 1980 the Swiss market share had collapsed to less than 10%, and its profit share dropped to less than 20%!

Discontinuous thinking turns a carburetor into a fuel injector. Discontinuous thinking turns a vinyl record into an eight-track tape, then an audiocassette, then a compact disc. What's next?

All innovative thinkers use discontinuous, "outside the nine dots" thinking. Join the club and reap the benefits!

Genius means little more than the faculty of

perceiving in an unhabitual way.

WILLIAM JAMES

Step 4. Ask questions no one else is asking, and then answer the questions creatively.

To get answers that no one else is getting, you must ask questions that no one else is asking. Ask, *"What one change, if it did happen, would revolutionize our industry?"* In addition, use the Innovation Questions you learned in Chapter 6.

1. **What if our company could _____?"**

2. **What if our company didn't have to _____?**

3. **What if our company could _____ and _____?**

4. **What if our customers could _____?**

5. **What if our customers didn't have to _____?**

6. **What if our customers could _____ and _____?**

Learning to ask these questions is the hardest part of Step 4, because, as you learned in Chapter 8, these questions open up files in your mind that haven't been opened in a while (or, more likely, have never been opened). But believe me, answering is easier than asking, because once a file is opened, the information in the file just comes pouring out.

Let me give you an example. Recently I did a training program for a corporation. I divided the group into teams of six people each and had them ask and answer the Step 4 questions. Here are a few of the questions and answers they created:

- *"**What if our company could** service our customers 24 hours a day, seven days a week?* Let's expand our help desk hours to 24 hours a day, seven days a week. That would give us an advantage over our competition, and may even decrease our costs, as the calls would be spread out over a longer period of time and we would need fewer answering stations."

- "It seems that we centralize our operations for a few years and then go on a decentralizing kick for a few years. *What if we could centralize **and** decentralize simultaneously?* Let's upgrade our computer network so that the home office gets instant feedback from the field (centralization), and those of us in the field can have access to all the information we need to make quick and accurate decisions out here (decentralization)."

- *"**What if our customers didn't have to** ever place an order?* Let's show our customers how we can handle their inventories better and less expensively than they can. We can be wired directly into a customer's inventory status at any given moment, and send out more product when their inventory reaches a predetermined level."

Step 5. Quickly take action on your creative ideas and keep what works.

The 3M Corporation has built a thriving business on taking action and keeping what works. 3M stands for Minnesota Mining and Manufacturing, because the company got its start around the turn of the century mining a resource called corundum. There was a lot of grit left over from their mining operations, so they used it to make sandpaper and grinding wheels. These auxiliary products quickly became the main profit center of the business!

3M continued to be on the lookout for new ideas. The company started making masking tape for the automotive paint industry when one of their salespeople overheard auto body painters complain about the difficulty of painting two-tone cars. When their customers asked for a waterproof packing tape, 3M built on the idea to create another product that has been fairly good to 3M—Scotch™ Tape. Nowadays, they create an adhesive for almost any purpose, including the product with the glue that doesn't work very well— Post-its. Today, 3M makes over 60,000 products! All because they take massive action on their ideas and keep what works.

Our company has, indeed, stumbled onto

some of its new products. But never forget

that you can only stumble if you're moving.

RICHARD P. CARLTON

FORMER CEO, 3M CORPORATION

Creating change is the most powerful tool you have in your toolbox. Your highest potential rewards come from creating change. If you don't have a lot of financial resources right now, remember that creativity itself is your most powerful resource! Creativity propelled Michael Dell from his University of Texas dorm room to the top echelon of computer companies. If you want to be a leader in any field, you will want to be an effective change creator.

Now let's apply the information in this chapter to creating change in your life by completing the Exercises for Action on the following pages.

EXERCISES FOR ACTION

1. Use the Six Steps for Creating Change in your Personal Life in the following exercises.

    A. Pick one unquestioned conviction you're currently holding in your personal life. Here are a few examples of unquestioned convictions: "I have to work in an office from nine to five in order to earn a living." "You have to have a college education in order to be successful." "A husband has to be the main breadwinner in a family." "I can't take time off from my career to have a baby or work from home once the baby arrives." The key is to search for a belief that is so strong you've never thought to question it. Write your unquestioned conviction in your journal.

    Now answer the following questions:

    *   *What* actions does this belief cause me to take or not to take?

    *   *Where* is this belief affecting my life negatively?

    *   *When* does this belief hinder me?

    *   With *whom* am I connected as a result of this belief? Does this belief truly support the relationship, or does it cause separation?

    *   *How* does this belief possibly hold me back from creating changes that will benefit me?

    *   *Why* not change now?

    If you decide this is a belief you would like to change, what new belief would you like to hold? Or how would you like to amend this belief to serve you and your life at a higher level? Write your new, amended belief in your journal. What will be the positive consequences of your new belief?

B. In your journal, list three ways you're committed to adding variety to your life, whether it be reading something new, taking up a new hobby or sport, visiting a new restaurant, or learning a new skill. For each item, give yourself a deadline to start this new activitiy, and make sure it is within the next two weeks.

C. Break the pattern of linear thinking! What's an example of a situation in which you must utilize cyclical thinking? Fashion? Your kids going back to school each year? A recurring cycle in your church or family? Where must you become aware of cycles in order to create change in your life?

What's an example of a situation in which you must utilize *parallel* thinking? Is there someone in your life you have to maintain two different kinds of relationships with—an employee who is also a friend, a son or daughter who is part of a soccer team you coach, your boss who is your doubles tennis partner? Where would it be to your advantage to utilize parallel thinking?

Where must you create change by utilizing *discontinuous* thinking? What changes do you need to plan for? Who or what won't be around forever? What kind of financial, legal, or emotional preparation do you need to make in order to handle potential disruptions in your life?

D. Pick a situation in which you would like to create change in your life. Answer the following questions about that situation. Do your best to come up with answers you've never gotten before!

- What if I could _____?

- What if I didn't have to _____?

- What if I could _____ *and* _____?

- What one change (if it did happen) would revolutionize my life in this area?

- What one or two changes in my life would move me closer to my dream?

E. Using the situation from D above, ask yourself, "Why is it absolutely vital that I make this change now?" Create a list of at least ten reasons you must create change in this particular area.

F. What actions will you take today to begin creating this change in your life?

2. Use the Five Steps for Creating Change in Your Business in the following exercises.

A. Pick one unquestioned conviction you're currently holding in your business. Here are a few examples: "All aspects of our business have to be under one roof." "Only management has the real overview and sense of how to run this company successfully. The employees just follow their directions." "We can't run this business 24 hours a day." (Or "We must stay open 24 hours a day to compete.") "It takes months to add a new product to our product line." The key is to search for a belief that is so strong you've never thought to question it. Write your unquestioned conviction in your journal.

Now, answer the following questions:

- *What* actions does this belief cause our company or business to take or not to take?

- *Where* is this belief affecting the company or business negatively?

- *When* does this belief hinder this company or business?

- With *whom* is this company connected as a result of this belief? Does this belief truly support the relationships within the company, with our vendors, and with our customers, or does it cause separation?

- *How* does this belief possibly hold the company back from creating changes that will benefit us?

- *Why* not change now?

If you decide this is a belief your company would like to change, what new belief would you like to hold? Or, how could your company amend this belief to serve your business and your customers at a higher level? Write the new, amended belief in your journal. What will be the positive consequences of this new belief?

B. Become more alert to innovative ideas occurring in your field and the world. How are you committed to adding more variety to the people and businesses you come into contact with? Where will you look for innovative ideas? In your journal, list three ways you will look for innovation and variety for your business, and next to each, give yourself a deadline.

C. Break the pattern of linear thinking! What's an example of a situation in which you must utilize cyclical thinking in your business? Are you phasing out one product while you phase another one in? Are there seasonal fluctuations you could take advantage of? Is your industry on an upswing or a downturn, and how could you stay ahead of the trend or buck the trend altogether? Where must you become aware of cycles in order to create change in your business?

What's an example of a situation in which you must utilize parallel thinking? Are you rolling out one product while developing another? How can you distinguish yourself from your competition by pursuing a completely different strategy and identity for your business? Are there parallel social trends (cocooning and adventure travel, for example) your company can take advantage of?

Where must you create change by utilizing discontinuous thinking? What products or services won't be needed in the future due to technological innovations? How can you creatively adapt your current business to take advantage of change in the years ahead? What kind of financial and legal preparation do you need to make in order to handle potential challenges to your business?

D. Pick a situation in which you would like to create change in your business. Answer the following questions about that situation. Do your best to come up with answers you've never gotten before!

- What if our company could _____?

- What if our company didn't have to _____?

- What if our company could _____ *and* _____?

- What if our customers could _____?

- What if our customers didn't have to _____?

- What if our customers could _____ *and* _____?

E. What actions can you take today to begin creating this change in your business?

We all belong to various groups, and all of them are affected by change. Leading group change, especially in the workplace, presents additional challenges for all Change Masters. In the next chapter, you will learn the leadership strategies that will enjoyably propel your group forward!

You'll learn the special strategies for . . .

Leading Group Change!

CHAPTER 14

Leading Group
Change

You're in a meeting with twenty of your colleagues at work. The CEO walks into the meeting five minutes late and announces, "Beginning tomorrow at this time, there are going to be some big changes made around here! I'll give you the details tomorrow— same time, same place!" He then turns around and walks out. What thoughts would be going through your mind over the next 24 hours?

The next day, the CEO walks into the meeting and states, "Remember the changes I mentioned yesterday? Here's what they are. Beginning today, we're going to change the color of all the office walls from white to beige!" If you're like most people, you would give a large sigh of relief because you assumed the big changes would be negative. This natural tendency to assume the worst is at the core of why leading group change can be so challenging.

In this chapter, you will learn the leadership strategies you can use to overcome negativity and thrust your business ahead in changing times. These same strategies can be reworked slightly and applied to leading change in any group.

Although many of the people I train work in large companies, this is not necessarily true of much of the business world. If you're an entrepreneur or an independent contractor, these same leadership skills are valuable in many settings. After all, you may find yourself on a "project team" as an outside consultant, vendor, or contractor. You may need to institute changes in your own small business, and want to help your clients and vendors understand the changes. You're probably going to be dealing with corporations, groups, or associations which are going through changes of some kind. You can use the skills and techniques presented here to help any group manage change.

These strategies will be presented using the Three Stages of Change Reaction framework you learned in Chapters 9, 10, and 11:

Stage 1: Letting Go of the Old

Stage 2: Transitioning Between the Old and the New

Stage 3: Embracing the New

Stage 1: Letting Go of the Old

All endings are difficult because they require leaving the familiar behind. Even when people logically see the need to make a change, they may resist emotionally because they are so used to swinging on that old trapeze bar with all of their friends. Any attempt to negate the process by skipping the stage of Letting Go of the Old, or pushing it along too quickly, will be met with active and/or passive resistance.

Leadership Strategies for Stage One

1. Communicate, communicate, communicate!

Remember Thriving on Change Belief #6—"I'm an active participant in the change process"? When people are actively involved in the change response process, they will react more resourcefully than if the process is just "dumped" on them.

Communication is the first component of active participation. Communicate early and often, in a variety of written and spoken forms. And remember, communication is a two-way street. Meet with your team often and solicit their input. And when they give it to you, listen! They usually know the most effective changes to be made because they are closest to the situations that need changing.

Control is the second component of active participation. Throughout all three stages of Change Reaction, give people as much control over the situation as realistically possible. If you don't do this, helplessness will settle in like a plague over your business, and helpless people shut down. Listen to your team and use their ideas in planning and enacting the Change Reaction process.

2. Clearly, concisely, and honestly communicate why this change is necessary.

Most Americans need to know the reason behind changes. We've been conditioned that way. It's one of our brain burps—it makes us feel more in control. I have a friend who tells a revealing story about a train trip she took in Europe. Below her window on the train was a sign that said, "Don't open the window," in several languages. All the different languages listed said the same thing, "Don't open the window," except the English line on the bottom. It said "Don't open the window because . . . " Some societies are just conditioned to want to know why things are the way they are!

Communicate the "whys" to your group in the following fashion: "In the past when things were like _____ in our industry, we could operate like _____. As I'm sure you've noticed, things have changed out there, and _____ has happened. As a result, _____ is our present situation. If we don't change, _____ is what it will be like in the future. We must make _____ changes now! _____ is what it will look like in the future when we do make these changes, and _____ is what it will mean you."

Here's an example: "In the past when we were the only widget-maker in our industry; we could set our own prices and couldn't manufacture widgets fast enough. As I'm sure you've noticed, things have changed in our industry, and we have a lot of competition from overseas widget makers. As a result, our present situation is that our products are priced much higher than our competitors', and we have a significant backlog of widgets sitting in our warehouses. If we don't change, in the future our client base will continue to shrink and we'll have to start laying off our manufacturing people within the next two months. We must make changes in both our production and distribution now! We have to lower our prices, and find a more efficient way to deliver our widgets to our customers quickly, without having to maintain an expensive supply of widgets here. What it will look like in the future when we do make these changes is we will be more responsive to our customers' needs and compete more aggressively in international markets. What it will mean to you is automating our production line more to reduce our costs, creating a new in-time delivery system that eliminates stockpiling product, and moving more people into international sales and marketing."

3. **Realize that every person is going to react to change in a unique way. Let your team know you understand what they're going through and you care about them.**

   Start by openly acknowledging any losses and how you feel personally. Do this in your printed communications and especially in your face-to-face encounters with individuals and groups. Make sure you always state the reason for the loss—if people remember there is a reason, often they will feel better (or at least not as threatened). For example, "Even though our restructuring is forcing us to reduce our team by 20%, I'm truly sorry that we are losing those people. They will be sorely missed!"

   Remember, each person will react to the change differently (and certainly differently than you are reacting to it) because each person has a different position, with different beliefs, expectations, obligations, resources, and goals. You must be especially flexible when dealing with people in times of change. Change—and the stress that goes with it—can create very unexpected and different reactions. Don't be surprised if you see "Sam Steady Producer" turn into "Sam I'm-Freaking-Out."

4. **Identify *what* is being lost and *who* is losing each of the "whats." Also, make a separate list of what is *not* being lost in this transition.**

   It is extremely important that you clearly communicate what is and *isn't* being lost. People need to know what they should *no longer be doing* (what's lost) and what they should *continue to do* (the things that are staying the same).

   Here's a great way to prepare to communicate clearly to your team. Divide a sheet of paper into three columns. In column one, make a list of precisely what is going to be lost—what is ending. Be thorough, honest, accurate, and specific! This is no time to beat around the bush. Each change may create other changes and other losses. Take the time to itemize what will be changing.

In a second column write who in your group is going to be losing each of the "whats" listed to the left. Some of the "whats" may be lost by everyone. Leave column three blank for now. (You'll learn how to create the solutions to these losses in Strategy #5.)

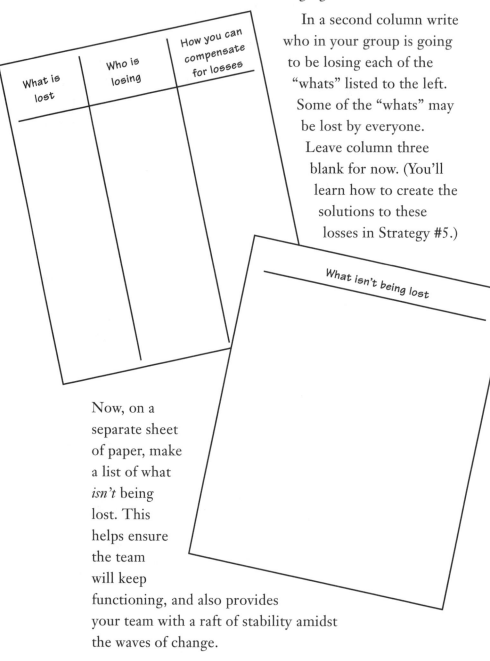

What is lost	Who is losing	How you can compensate for losses

What isn't being lost

Now, on a separate sheet of paper, make a list of what *isn't* being lost. This helps ensure the team will keep functioning, and also provides your team with a raft of stability amidst the waves of change.

5. **Let people know they will be compensated for their losses whenever possible.**

   In the third column of the "what is being lost" list you started (the list of precisely what is going to be lost and who is losing it), write all the ways you can compensate people for their losses. Make sure you're compensating them in the same areas where they feel the losses. If they're losing their jobs, let them know you're going to help them find new ones. If they're moving to a new position within the company and are feeling a lack of technical skills required to do the new job, let them know they will receive training for their new position.

   If they're moving to a different area in your facility and are going to miss the daily contact with their friends, tell them where they will be and all the ways they can develop friendships in their new area. You might even want to set up a "let's get to know each other" lunch.

   It may not be possible to compensate people for every single effect of this change, but it's important to make sure that every point on your list has been addressed, and people have a general sense that efforts will be made to support them during the change process.

6. **Honor the past, clearly mark the break with the old, and create a vision of the future that inspires people to action.**

   Even if you're new to the team, never make the past wrong. Instead, convey the concept, "The immediate past was another leg in the journey that has brought us to where we are now." Recognize the efforts of the team thus far. Find something good to say. Even if the results were not what was needed, you can always honor the intentions of the team.

   Next, you need to assert that, starting now, there is going to be a definite break with the old. You can mark the break with *time* ("Today we begin the new Chrysler!"), a change in *facilities* (a new office layout), a change in *process* (a new distribution system), a change in *principles* ("Here is the new set of guiding principles upon which this company will be run!"), etc.

Share your excitement about what these changes will create for the team. Let them see, hear, feel, taste, and smell what the new company is going to be like. In this stage, don't be too surprised if they aren't as excited as you are about your vision for the future! They may be preoccupied with the ever-changing present. As a leader, it's your responsibility to offer them a new possibility that will begin to move them away from the old and toward the future they need to create.

Remember, Stage One is designed simply to help your team let go of the old ways of doing, thinking, and feeling. If you've done your job right, at the minimum everyone should feel that they personally, along with the entire team, are a part of the process of change. They should feel their concerns have been addressed, their voices have been heard, and everything possible has been done to manage the process of change successfully. Then they will be ready to let go and look positively toward the future.

Stage 2: Transitioning Between the Old and the New

Transitioning between the old and the new can be either confusing and dangerous, or it can be a time of great creativity and innovation because there are fewer and weaker ties to both the old and the new. Group change turns up the heat under your boiling pot. Don't let this dynamic energy get away from you or oppress you. Harness it properly, and you'll guide your group to new heights!

Confusion is a word we have invented

for an order which is not yet understood.

HENRY MILLER

Leadership Strategies for Stage Two

1. **Keep the effective two-way communication going, and keep your team involved in the process by providing them with an important role to play.**

    The more your team is involved in this time of transition, the more in control and assured they will feel. Plus, they may have ideas or insights that would never occur to you, because they're closer to the front lines than you are!

2. **Create a theme for the transition period that suggests a journey from one stage to another.**

    One way people make sense of their lives is through metaphors. A "sinking ship" metaphor doesn't empower people. A journey from one port to another is a metaphor that does.

People use metaphors unconsciously all the time. Listen for the metaphors your team is using, and make sure you create some powerful ones to guide them through the transition phase. If you wish, borrow the trapeze metaphor I used in Chapters 9, 10, and 11. Use your chosen metaphors consistently whenever you communicate with your team. You may even want to represent these metaphors graphically in your written communication—have some fun!

3. **Create support systems for the transition period.**

Review your policies and procedures, and make sure they deal adequately with all the changes occurring in the transition stage. New roles, reporting relationships, and titles may need to be created in this stage.

It's important to set easily achievable short-term goals to give people a sense of accomplishment. In times of transition, people often feel they are working toward an unclear future and not getting concrete results fast enough. A lot of what they are doing may be laying the groundwork for big payoffs down the road. It's important to make sure that there are goals and rewards at every stage of the transition so people can feel a sense of progress and personal accomplishment every step along the way.

You may need to provide appropriate training to give people the additional skills they need to succeed in this challenging time. It's an investment that will produce big rewards for your team in the long run.

4. **Create high levels of team synergy.**

Use newsletters, weekly lunches, company picnics, and special celebration parties to create synergy. Let people know, "We're all in this together." People will endure a lot when they're part of a team where everyone is making sacrifices and contributions. Wander around the office, and make a point of connecting with people. It'll make your team stronger daily!

5. Create a Transition Facilitation Team.

This team will facilitate the upward and downward communication of information through the grapevine. This will not only make sure the information you want disseminated is put out there effectively, but it will also enroll your team members more deeply in the process of change. And when people feel involved, they feel invested!

6. Provide a safety net for the people who may need it.

First, keep your word: Make sure you compensate your team's losses according to the plan you jointly developed in Stage One. It's especially important for morale that people who leave the company or team are seen to have been treated fairly and with respect.

You also need to make sure the rest of the team is taken care of. Many companies that have undergone extensive changes (including a reduction in total number of employees) have reported that the people who *remained* had more emotional challenges than those who were no longer with the company.

While some kinds of emotional challenges should be handled quite effectively by this three-stage change management process, making more individualized support available as well is a good idea. An Employee Assistance Program is a valuable addition in times of rapid change. Let your team know that getting help in managing the stress of transition is not only okay, but it's also a smart thing to do.

Stage 3: Embracing the New

Once you've helped your team let go of the old and supported them in their transition between the old and the new, you can assist them to embrace the new. Show your team how to catch the new bar—in time, they'll actually enjoy swinging on it!

Leadership Strategies for Stage Three

1. **Clearly and passionately communicate your corporate vision and what needs to happen as you move toward that vision as a team.**

   This is the time to emphasize your corporate vision. Your people have gone through the first two stages, and now they are ready to listen. Visions inspire enthusiastic action.

   Communicate to everyone what the vision will look, sound, and feel like. Repeatedly show, tell, and provide references from other organizations that have successfully made similar changes. Use any impactful method available to convey to your team what this future will be like. And make sure you communicate the purpose behind your corporate vision. Your people want to know the "why" behind your vision.

   Your people will also want to know what's in it for them. Tell them! Make sure they know the specific rewards these changes will bring and how rapidly you foresee these rewards accruing.

2. **Communicate the step-by-step plan for the achievement of this new vision.**

   Now that your group clearly sees the vision and understands why movement toward the vision is essential, they are ready for the plan. When traveling on an unfamiliar road toward a vision, people feel much better when they can see a road map between point A and point B. Lay your plan

out, and get input from your team. The more involved they
are in creating the road map, the more enthusiastic
their efforts will be!

3. Create a valuable role for every member of your team in the achievement of the vision.

Empower your people to be active participants all along
the way in creating solutions for challenges. This will give
them a sense of control that enrolls them in the process.
Let them know constantly how valuable they are, both
individually and as a team.

4. Celebrate your wins every step along the way.

Make sure there are a few wins immediately. As Ken
Blanchard says, "Catch people doing things right!" Your team
needs instant reinforcement whenever they have accomplished
something new successfully. That way, they'll develop the
confidence to move ahead to more challenging tasks.

Keep recognizing and celebrating victories at every stage
of the change process. In the circus, every time someone
catches the bar, the audience applauds! As the leader of change
for your team, make sure you follow the same principle.
Personally and in public, recognize the contributions made by
individuals and the entire team. Post notices and print articles
in your company newsletter to celebrate accomplishments.
Have parties that are joyous celebrations of progress. Make
sure everyone knows how their successes are contributing
to the new vision!

Throughout All Three Stages

As the Change Leader, there are a few additional pointers
to keep in mind.

1. **Realize people start their personal change processes at
   different times.**

   As a leader, your start time will be sooner than your associates'.
   You will know about the internal changes before they do.
   Make sure you communicate rapidly and appropriately.
   Don't assume your team is "in the know."

2. **Realize people go through their personal change
   processes at different speeds.**

   As a leader, you may travel faster than they do. Make sure
   you "catch them up" whenever possible. You can't lead a
   team if you're so far ahead they can't see you anymore!

3. **Realize everyone is going to react to change differently.**

   As a leader, you may react more resourcefully than they do.
   Help people access the resources they already have inside.
   Above all, don't let helplessness set in. Keep people involved!

4. **Communicate, communicate, communicate!**

   Don't hide out in your office because you believe people
   don't want to hear "negative" information, or because you
   don't want to be the bearer of "bad" news. Your people
   want to know what's going on and will hear it anyway—
   probably in a negative, exaggerated form.

5. **Even more important than talking with your team,
   make sure you're listening to them.**

   Even if there are some painful aspects of the change
   process that you can't do anything about, just hearing
   someone out will often make them feel better. Your door

should always be open to every team member, and they should feel that you are a fair, open, and helpful leader who will be there for them as part of the team.

6. Remember—you're human, too.

It may be true that "the buck stops here," and you may have to make some difficult decisions affecting people's lives. You can't do it all yourself. Luckily, you don't have to—that's one of the advantages of a team. Listen with your head and your heart to your team's input. They have answers to questions that you never would have thought to ask.

To learn more about leading change at work, I recommend William Bridges's *Managing Transitions—Making the Most of Change* and Daryl Conner's *Managing at the Speed of Change*.

You've done it! You and your team have successfully made the transition and entered into a new stage of growth and expansion for your business. Now, let's apply the information in this chapter to all the groups in your life by doing the Exercises for Action on the following pages.

EXERCISES FOR ACTION

1. Think of a change you need to make as part
    of a group, either in your business or your
    personal life. Using the steps outlined in this
    chapter, create an action plan to facilitate
    change in your group.

Stage 1: Letting Go of the Old

1. How do you plan to communicate clearly, concisely,
    and honestly with the group why this change is
    necessary?

2. How will you let each person on your team know
    you understand what they're going through and
    you care about them?

3. Identify what is being lost, and who is losing it.

4. How will you honor the past, making sure your
    team knows you recognize the efforts of the team
    thus far?

5. How will you clearly mark the break with the old,
    using either time, facilities, or principles?

6. How will you create and communicate your vision
    of the future to your team so they are inspired to
    take action?

Stage 2: Transitioning Between the Old and the New

1. How will you keep the two-way communication going between you and your team? What role will you ask them to play?

2. What theme will you create for the transition period that suggests a journey from one stage to another?

3. What support systems must you create for this transition period?

4. How will you increase the level of team synergy? What tools (newsletters, weekly gatherings, celebrations, etc.) will you use to keep you and your team excited and connected?

5. Who will be on your Transition Facilitation Team, and what actions will they be expected to take?

6. What safety net will be provided to those who need it?

Stage 3: Embracing the New

1. How will you clearly and passionately communicate your vision and what needs to happen as you all move toward that vision as a team?

2. What is your step-by-step plan for achieving the vision, and how will you communicate it?

3. What role will each team member play in the achievement of the vision?

4. How will you celebrate your wins every step along the way?

The last six chapters have been loaded with powerful strategies for utilizing change to your advantage. In the next section, "Your Place in the Next Millennium," you will discover a few paths you might want to consider taking, and how to handle the challenges you will certainly face along the way. Read on. Your destiny awaits you!

Discover how to create . . .

Your Place in the New Millennium!

Your Place in
the New Millenium

It's New Year's Eve 2009. In one hour the new millennium will be ten years old! Where will you be in your life? What will you be doing, and with whom? How much change will have occurred in the world between today and the year 2010, and what will be your place in it? Did you stick your head in the sand and not even see the changes? Did you stand in front of the steamroller of change and demand that it stop moving—and get flattened by it? Did you sit on the beach and just watch the changes? Did the waves of change turn you head-over-heels?

Or did you *anticipate* the changes and ride them successfully? Did you *create* change and surf triumphantly on a wave of your own making?

As you learned in Section Two, the answers to these questions will be determined by

- the *principles* upon which you base your life;

- the *habits* those principles foster;

- the *beliefs* you hold about your changing world, the people in it, and yourself;

- the *strategies* you use to take advantage of change.

In the first three sections, you learned how to react to, anticipate, and create change both for yourself and in groups. In this section, you will take everything you've learned so far, and apply it to your own unique path through life.

Get ready to master . . .

Creating Success in the 21st Century!

Creating Success in the 21st Century

Back in the '60s and '70s, your job security was based on the company you worked for. If you worked for a company like IBM, General Motors, or Control Data, people said, "Wow, are you lucky! You're set for life!" Things have definitely changed today! Your job security does not lie in the company you work for. It lies in your ability to provide value—in the skills you possess.

As you should realize from all the business examples I've given so far, it's not enough anymore merely to have a job, because the odds are a hundred to one that your job will either vanish or completely change in the years ahead. You need to focus your energies not on being employed, but instead on being *employable*—having the skills that will compel employers to want you on their team.

The rapid change in the world today is definitely bringing back a healthy dose of self-reliance. Today, your only real competitive advantage

is your ability to learn faster than other people in the work force.
**Constant and rapid learning is necessary to move ahead in today's
business world.** There's another, equally vital personal reason to be a
lifelong learner: **People are happiest when they're learning and
growing.** Think of a time when you felt like you were "stuck" in your
life. Were you happy? Now think of a time when you were truly
happy. Were you learning and growing?

The same principle works just as well for entire companies.
In the 21st century, the only real advantage your company will have is
its ability to learn faster than the competition. Businesses and people
who want to *earn* more must constantly and consistently *learn* more.
The companies that learn and grow the fastest will thrive in the years
ahead. Those that don't, won't!

The following three graphs illustrate this point.

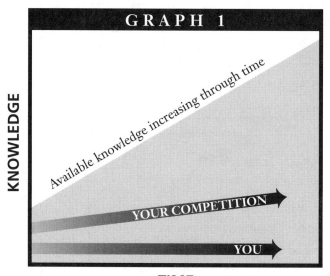

Graph 1 shows what happens when you (or your company)
aren't actively learning. You might think your learning level is staying
the same, but unless you're making an active effort to gain knowledge
continuously, you won't keep up with the world around you. Just by
staying in the same place, you're falling behind—you're losing
knowledge in relation to the total amount of knowledge available!

To make things even more compelling, your worldwide competition is constantly *gaining* knowledge. In Graph 1, notice how the gap between you, your competition, and all available knowledge increases over time. This gap will eventually be reflected in your paycheck (or your company's bottom line). If you've ever felt like you're losing ground at work or in your personal life, you know what I'm talking about!

Graph 2 shows what happens when you're learning at the same rate as your competition. You improve, but you gain no ground.

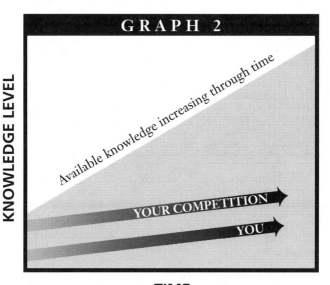

Graph 3 reveals what it takes to get ahead today. You must learn *faster* than the competition—whether your competition is around the corner or around the globe.

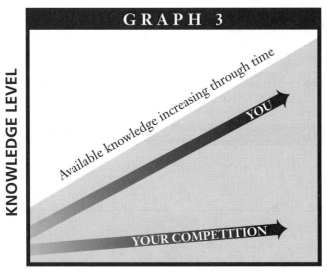

Remember, competition isn't just about creating winners and losers. Healthy competition, in the long run, will stimulate everyone to learn and grow!

Now that you're inspired to accelerate your own learning curve, here are three resources you will want to utilize constantly.

1. Motivation

This is the engine that drives all change. One of the best ways to be motivated is to get associated to what you'll *lose* if you don't learn and grow, and what you'll *gain* if you do. So take a few moments to get motivated. In your journal or on a sheet of paper, write your answers to the following questions.

- What will it *cost* me emotionally and financially if I don't make learning and growing a priority?

- What will I *gain* emotionally and financially by making learning and growing a priority in my life?

Learning and growing are essential if you're going to thrive on change. If you're not motivated to do so by now, we need to talk!

2. Time

When it comes right down to it, you and I make time for what's truly important to us. I hope your happiness and success are important to you.

In a television commercial for California almonds, the almond growers said, "A can of almonds a week. That's all we ask." I'm asking you to invest at least *four hours a week* in learning and growing in ways that will make a difference in your life.

The old saying "if you want a job done, give it to a busy person" applies here, too. If you're busy, congratulations! You're ready to begin spending more time learning and growing.

Where will the time come from? Take a look at how much TV you watch. The average adult in the U.S. watches five hours of TV a day! Consider cutting your TV time in half and using the extra time to learn and grow.

You can also use new technologies to save time. My computer with its modem, portable printer, and contact management system must save me at least six hours a week. So make the commitment to investing time in your future now, and write it in your journal.

The amount of time I am committed to invest in learning and growing is _____ hour(s) per week.

---

3. Money

One of the premier consulting firms in the U.S., Andersen Consulting, spends 6% of its gross income on training, an extraordinarily high percentage. The average Andersen employee is in the classroom 135 hours a year! You should do the same in your own life, even if your company doesn't supply the training. If you run a company, you should provide that level of training for your employees. Remember, your only sustainable advantage both personally and professionally is your ability to learn faster than your competition. So invest first in your own growth—the dividends will beat even the highest Wall Street return!

Make the commitment to invest your capital in your future growth, and make a note of your decision.

> **The amount of money I am committed to invest in**
> **learning and growing is $_____ per year.**

Now that you're committed, here are six suggestions for profitable ways to invest your time and money.

1. Read books.

One of the best ways to "take a rich person to lunch" is by reading their books. You can compress years into hours by reading books written by people who have done things you want to do, or know things you want to know. It's also great to read autobiographies and biographies of people you admire. This is the best way to get into the minds of these great people, to learn the principles, habits, beliefs, and strategies that formed the foundation for their successes.

Remember what I said at the beginning of this book: The average American reads less than one nonfiction book per year, and 58% of all Americans never read a nonfiction book after high school! If you read only one nonfiction book a month, you will be in the top 1% of adult learners. If you read just one nonfiction book a *week*, you will have read five hundred books in ten years, which will put you in the top 0.1% of adult learners!

2. Listen to audiotapes.

Audiotapes are a superb way to gain information without spending any additional time. How? The average person spends five hundred to a thousand hours in his or her car every year. This equates to 12.5 to 25 forty-hour work weeks! If you listened to audiotapes only half the time you're in the car, you could be in school six to twelve weeks each year. Audiotapes have another advantage over books—you get to hear the emotion and power that lie behind the author's words.

3. Attend live training programs, courses, seminars, and workshops.

Live programs are often the best learning vehicles because you get to see, hear, and feel the experience, and you can ask questions of the expert. I recommend you attend at least three days of live trainings every year. Remember, the Andersen Consulting people are in the classroom an average of 135 hours yearly.

To stretch as a person, you need to get outside your comfort zone every once in a while. A personal development program that helps you examine and improve your life as a whole is an excellent idea. Good experiential programs will do this for you, and I believe those offered by Anthony Robbins are some of the finest available. You might want to check out the Anthony Robbins programs described at the end of this book.

4. Watch educational television or videotapes.

There are hundreds of cable and satellite programs and video-tapes available. Turn your living room into a classroom.

5. Use interactive programs on your computer.

Of all the methods mentioned so far, this may be the easiest and most accessible way to learn. Right now I'm learning Spanish and my daughter is improving her math and reasoning skills with CD-ROM interactive programs.

6. Talk with people who have done what you want to do.

There is nothing better than sitting down with someone and getting the benefit of their experience. Be sure you give something in return for their time (e.g., buy them lunch).

Your learning should fall into three categories:

1) directly related to your job or profession (e.g., a seminar in your particular field)

2) indirectly related to your job or profession (a time management program, for example)

3) completely unrelated to your business life (perhaps a weekend gardening course, or learning how to skydive).

Expand your boundaries! Read or listen to some material that will stretch you personally and professionally. Attend an off-beat program or two. Regularly talk to people who hold outlandish views. Remember, if you keep doing the same things and talking to the same people, you will keep getting the same results. As Tom Peters says, "Crazy times call for crazy corporations and crazy people!" The lesson is obvious—get crazy every once in a while!

I can't tell you exactly what, where, and how to invest your time and money because I don't know where you are now or where you want to go. You need to ask, **"What knowledge and skills do I need *right now* to continue my journey toward my personal vision?"** Your personal vision is the future you want to create—your personal dream of everything you want to be, do, have, and give. Dreams give power and passion to your everyday activities. They wake you up early and keep you up late as you transform your personal dream into a reality. To paraphrase Oscar Hammerstein, you gotta have a dream to make a dream come true!

Dreams act like a homing beacon—they direct you to *do* the things that move you closer to your dream. In order to *have* your dream, you must do certain things; in order to *do* certain things you must *be* a certain kind of person. And as a result of *being* that kind of person, you will *give* your best to yourself, to others, and ultimately, to the world.

Let me give you an example. Right now my son Chris and daughter Emily are working toward university degrees. Chris is going for a master's in public policy, and Emily is earning a bachelor's in architectural history. Their dreams include the degrees they will earn as well as all the doors those degrees will open for them and the contributions they will make to the world as a result. But in order for them to make those contributions, they need to *have* a degree; in order to have a degree, they have to *do* certain things—go to class, study, do term papers, take tests, etc. In order for them to do these things, they have to *be* motivated, intelligent, flexible, focused. My point? It all starts with *being*.

It's the same with doing, having, and giving the things you desire in your rapidly changing world. You will have to cultivate nine traits, nine ways of being, in order to become a master of change.

The Nine Traits of Personal Change Mastery

1. Be grounded.

Live a life based on the universal principles you read about in Chapter 3. These universal principles will act as the roots that will hold your tree into the earth even in the strongest of winds.

2. Be a master of change utilization.

Know how to react to, anticipate, create, and lead change. Don't hide from, fight, or just cope with change. Use change to masterfully build a life and a legacy that will make you proud and the world better. I hope this book will be your guide to successfully utilizing change in the years ahead.

3. Be flexible.

In addition to their root
systems, the other reason trees
can withstand strong winds is
flexibility. No matter what direction
the wind comes from, or how fast it
blows, a tree bends in just the right way
to accept the challenge. After the storm
subsides, the tree uses its flexibility to
stand straight and tall again.

You need flexibility in your personal life and in the way you
approach your work. From 1982 to 1992, the total work force in the
U.S. increased 20%. In that same time period, the temporary work
force increased 250%! Remember, the Department of Labor estimates
that less than half of the workers in the U.S. will be holding conventional full-time jobs in the year 2000.

One of the great advantages of the coming millennium will be
increased flexibility in our choice of where to live. According to Paul
Pilzer, in the next twenty years sixty to seventy million people will
move from the suburbs to the "exurbs"—locations far away from
the central cities. More and more of my friends are moving to places
like Bend, Oregon, Hamilton, Montana, and Iowa City, Iowa, and
conducting their businesses by phone, fax, and modem.

Finally, you need to be flexible in the way you interact with others
both personally and professionally. Our rapidly changing world is
bringing diverse cultures closer together than ever. You may find yourself working side by side with someone from Mexico or Taiwan, calling
Australia to set up a business, or having e-mail relationships with friends
from Denmark or Russia. Each culture has its own set of rules and taboos,
and you need to be sensitive and flexible in your communication.
You'll find the rewards of cross-cultural friendships are enormous!

4. Be a lifetime learner.

Take another hint from the trees—they're growing until the day they die. Be curious! Use modeling, plussing, innovation, and reinvention (Chapter 6) to create a life that's an evolving masterpiece.

We live in the age of knowledge creation and information transfer. The information supply available to you doubles every five years. To stay an active participant in this age, you must constantly do your homework. Think of yourself as a machine with a five-year lifespan. In five years, your business and personal skills must be almost 100% reinvented.

If you work in a corporation, you will want to think in terms of *horizontal* movement, not the traditional vertical movement up the corporate ladder. Even in the corporate world, think of yourself as an entrepreneur or independent consultant. As Tom Peters says, "Move from one neat project to another." Think, "What can I learn?" not "Where can I go?"

5. Be a master information processor.

In 1950, 73% of the employees in the U.S. worked in manufacturing or production. In 1994, that figure was less than 15%, and it will drop even further in the years ahead. Most new jobs in the future will be in collecting, processing, and communicating information. You must learn to use these new information processing technologies to ride your turbo-charged racer on the information highway!

At the absolute minimum, you should have a personal computer with CD-ROM capability at home as a learning aid for you and your family. If necessary, sell your TV and buy a personal computer!

One of the great advantages of being a master information processor is the freedom it gives you. Many people have left the nine to five corporate world to strike out on their own. They have used their skills to set up businesses based from home or from their own office. Often they may work with the same corporation they were employed by in the past, but they make more money and have greater flexibility in scheduling. Whether you decide to stay in the corporate world or create your own business, it's essential your skills and resources are focused upon the ability to collect and process information.

6. Be a world player.

Vastly improved communication and transportation are making our world smaller; world economic alliances, sports, and cultural events are making it feel closer. You must be an active component of that smaller, tighter world. Read about world events on a regular basis. Learn another country's language and culture. What happens in other parts of the world will have a greater and greater impact on your life, so keep yourself up to date.

7. Be a team player.

As our world becomes more interconnected and interdependent, teams are becoming more important in business and your daily life. Your ability to form effective teams, synergistically work in teams by providing tremendous value to your teammates, and occasionally lead those teams, will contribute heavily to your success and enjoyment in the years ahead. My friend Brian Biro's fabulous book, *Beyond Success*, is an excellent resource on the power of team.

8. Be a master of creativity.

Your ability to solve problems creatively, utilize change, and generate new ideas will be increasingly valuable in the next millennium. Use your creativity to produce numerous plusses and innovations in your business and your life. Keep thinking outside the nine dots!

9. Be unique.

As the world gets smaller and more competitive, you will want to be more unique so that you stand out in the crowd. Like MCI and Southwest Airlines, you will want to create a personality and set of life skills that will get you noticed and produce results no one else can produce!

Just as there are nine keys to achieving success personally in the next millennium, here are nine traits your company should have to thrive in the years ahead.

The Nine Traits of Change Mastery in Business

1. Build your company on universal principles.

A company with no ethical foundation is like a house of cards, toppled by the slightest of winds. A company built on universal principles can withstand the strongest gale!

2. Create a learning corporation.

The number one asset of most corporations today is the cumulative knowledge of its employees. In 1992, Nintendo had $5.5 billion in sales and $1.3 billion in pre-tax profits. Nintendo did it with 892 employees—an average of $6 million in sales per employee per year! Nintendo's advantage is not buildings, equipment, or other physical "stuff." It lies in the ability to use the knowledge of its employees to build great games.

Do you know what a state-of-the-art $600 camera is composed of? $2 worth of plastic, $20 of optical glass—and $578 of knowledge. Knowledge is your company's number one resource! Tom Peters is right when he urges every corporation to have a Director of Knowledge Management. Your only true competitive advantage in the years ahead will be your ability to learn faster than your competition.

There are three components of a learning corporation:

- A *compelling corporate vision* that literally pulls the corporation and its people to success

- A *motivated group of people* who each have a personal vision that is in alignment with the corporate vision

- A *creative and nurturing environment* that helps everyone enjoyably move toward their visions

3. Master change utilization.

As change comes along and levels the playing field in your industry, it's vital that you use change to your company's advantage. When a change occurs in your industry, ask yourself, "What are the opportunities here?" and "How are my company and I going to have to change in response to this new situation?" (See the chapters in Section 3 for concrete steps to utilize change effectively.)

4. Make flexibility a priority.

Businesses that thrive in times of rapid change are strong in their adherence to universal principles and extremely flexible in the strategies they use to move ahead. You hear a lot these days about the "virtual corporation." A virtual corporation constantly and quickly changes form. It utilizes an ever-changing array of internal resources and outsources much of its work. The virtual corporation forms alliances with its customers, suppliers, other corporations, and even its competitors, to uniquely give its customers exactly what they want, where they want it, when they want it.

Harry Dent says successful corporations are transforming from whales into schools of minnows. Astute CEOs like Microsoft's Bill Gates are constantly shaking things up in their organizations to make sure that "hardening of the processes" doesn't take place. Flexible organizations are the ones that will thrive in the future. In the U.S. between 1987 and 1991, the Fortune 500 companies laid off 2.4 million workers. Companies of twenty or fewer employees added 4.4 million jobs!

Small companies—and large companies that act like small companies—are usually the most flexible, and they are thriving as a result.

Remember, be flexible with your strategies, but never change the foundational principles and habits that made your company what it is today.

5. Constantly improve so that you can deliver superb quality and thrill the customer.

The best corporations are constantly improving their people, processes, products, and services. They know that they can never rest on their laurels. They use plussing and innovation to constantly stay ahead of the competition, and they re-engineer as needed.

The greatest key to long-term profitability is quality as it is perceived by the customer. These days, excellent service only gets you into the game. Today's consumers demand unique products and services of exceptional quality backed by world-class service, creating an experience that thrills and delights. And the standard will only keep getting higher.

To move ahead, you must thrill the customer—give them even more than they expect. I love to fly on Southwest Airlines because they consistently give me much more than I expect. I just received a birthday card from them that said, "Please remain celebrating until the party has come to a complete stop. Best wishes on your birthday from all of us at Southwest Airlines." How many other airlines send their frequent flier customers birthday cards? Answer: None!

6. Utilize new technologies.

Effectively utilizing the newest technologies will be critical if your company is to survive in the new millennium. Keep abreast of the latest innovations in your industry and related fields. Make it a priority to implement new technology as often as possible. If you don't know how to use something, find out quickly!

Pizza Hut is an example of a company thriving in part because they utilize new technologies. When you call to order a pizza, the complete information on your pizza ordering history (when you ordered, how many and what size pizzas you ordered, what toppings you requested, and your exact delivery address) pops up on a computer screen in front of the order taker. He or she then can ask you, "Did you want mushrooms with that this time, or do you just want to have the green pepper and extra garlic?" Pizza Hut knows more about your pizza preferences than anyone! And they use that information very effectively to help you order more of their product.

7. Create a unique identity for your company.

In today's highly-competitive marketplace, you can't be all things to all people. You will want to concentrate on being one or two unique things to a few people. As Michael Treacy and Fred Wiersema say in their excellent book, *The Discipline of Market Leaders*, you must choose your customers and narrow your focus. When you do that, *and* you provide a collection of unique and high-quality products/services, you can dominate your segment of the marketplace.

8. Focus on customization.

When I was growing up, there were four flavors of ice cream— vanilla, chocolate, strawberry, and (if you really got wild) butter brickle. Now there are hundreds of flavors, including Ben and Jerry's Cherry Garcia and Chubby Hubby. There used to be only two kinds of life insurance products—term and whole life. Now there are dozens of choices. You used to have to buy your shoes off the shelf, and you got a pair that fit—sort of. Now, thanks to brand-new software, you can go to a Custom Foot store, where your foot is measured in fourteen different ways by electronic scanner. Then you choose your shoe style, type, grade of leather, color, lining, and so on, from displays on a computer screen. All these instructions are transmitted (in Italian!) to shoemakers in Italy, who make your shoes and ship them back to the U.S., usually within two or three weeks of your order. All of this for about $99 to $250, the price of a good, non-custom-made pair of shoes!

We're moving from a standardized economy to a customized economy. You need to hop on the customization bandwagon!

9. Focus on the growth areas of our economy.

There are certain areas of our economy that are sure to grow in the coming years. They include:

- *Information collecting, processing, and communicating*— The Information Revolution will be exactly that.

- *Adult education*—Retraining adults to help them keep up with a changing world will be a huge industry in the years ahead.

- Anything that will *save people time*—Remember when you were growing up, the "experts" forecast that we would all be working a thirty-hour work week in the future? They were partially right. Half of us are working sixty-hour work weeks, and the other half are unemployed! The half who are working sixty hours have the money, and will spend it on almost anything that will help them save time.

- *Health care*—As the Baby Boomers age, the demand for health care will drastically increase, as will the range of health care services needed. Providing and managing health care will be a huge industry for years to come.

- Anything that will make the Baby Boomers *look or feel younger*—Whitening toothpaste, health club equipment, waist cinchers—we're so vain!

- *Personal services*—Services such as fitness trainers and personal shoppers will be in demand, providing both time-saving and customized services to busy Boomers.

- Anything *unique culturally* (especially when marketed globally)—Coke, Disney, Levis, Evian, and NBA basketball are examples of products already thriving in the world marketplace.

- Anything that will help the *environment*—As the impact of global pollution continues to rise, the "greening of the world" will also continue.

Oliver Wendell Holmes once said, "The greatest thing in this world is not so much *where* we are, but in what direction we are moving." I don't know where you are in your life right now, but I do know one thing for sure: It isn't the same place you'll be in five years. Our rapidly changing world won't let that happen. If necessary, it will move *around* you to produce a new place for you in the changed world. The $64,000 question is, "Are you going to move in the right direction, at the right speed, at the right time to create your own unique niche?"

Napoleon Hill once said, "It's always your next move." This chapter has given you eighteen useful guidelines to help you plan your personal and business "next move." This is the part of life where the real challenge and excitement begins. This is the part of life that smart, flexible, and quick people relish. This is the part of life where dreams are created! Make your next move right now by completing this chapter's Exercises for Action!

EXERCISES FOR ACTION

1. Re-examine Your Change Mastery Skills

Let's try an experiment. Answer the same question you did in Chapter 1:

What meaning do I draw from all the changes occurring in my world today?

In your answer, consider how the changes are affecting you, as well as your degree of participation in the process.

Now analyze your answer on the following two scales. On a scale of –10 to +10, with –10 being extremely negative, 0 being neutral, and +10 being extremely positive, where does your answer fall?

Extremely Negative										Neutral										Extremely Positive
–10	–9	–8	–7	–6	–5	–4	–3	–2	–1	0	+1	+2	+3	+4	+5	+6	+7	+8	+9	+10

On a scale of –10 to +10, with –10 being, "I'm a victim of change. There's nothing I can do about it," 0 being neutral, and +10 being, "I'm an active participant in the change process," where does your answer fall?

Victim										Neutral										Active Participant
–10	–9	–8	–7	–6	–5	–4	–3	–2	–1	0	+1	+2	+3	+4	+5	+6	+7	+8	+9	+10

Now compare these answers with those from page 10 in Chapter 1. How have they changed? If you have read this book with your heart as well as your mind, I'm sure your scores have moved into, or are closer to, the +4 to +8 range that I see in people who consistently thrive on change.

2. Look at the nine traits you need to possess to thrive in the years ahead. Construct a blueprint for your learning and growing over the course of the next six months to a year. Even if you have limited resources, get started with some kind of a plan right now! How will you . . .

1. **be grounded?**

2. **be a master of change utilization?**

3. **be flexible?**

4. **be a lifetime learner?**

5. **be a master information processor?**

6. **be a world player?**

7. **be a team player?**

8. **be a master of creativity?**

9. **be unique?**

3. Look at the nine traits your business should focus on to thrive in the years ahead. Construct a blueprint to transform your organization over the next six months to a year. Even if you have limited resources, get started with some kind of a plan right now! How will you . . .

1. **build your company on universal principles?**

2. **create a learning corporation?**

3. **master change utilization?**

4. **make flexibility a priority?**

5. **constantly improve so that you can deliver superb quality and thrill the customer?**

6. **utilize new technologies?**

7. **create a unique identity for your company?**

8. **focus on customization?**

9. **focus on the growth areas of our economy?**

Rapid change is like a stiff wind—if you're not prepared, it can blow you over. If you are prepared, you can use its power to lift you to the heavens!

Read on to learn the art of . . .

Soaring Into Your Future!

Soaring Into Your Future

An eagle can fly horizontally at about forty miles per hour. What's the only thing holding the eagle back from flying faster? The air resistance, right? How fast do you think the eagle could fly if there were no air resistance in its face—fifty, sixty, seventy miles per hour?

Actually, *without air resistance it couldn't fly at all*. No air resistance means no air. The eagle would be in a vacuum, and would fall to the ground. The resistance is the very thing that the eagle uses to soar. The air is simultaneously in the eagle's face and flowing over its wings to lift it toward the heavens!

The air resistance is both the eagle's challenge and its necessity for flight. The same is true with the challenges created by change. These challenges are the very things you must use to soar!

Adversity reveals genius; prosperity conceals it.

HORACE

That's why this book is called *Thriving on Change*. Changes create challenges, and thriving on these challenges is the spice of life. If you had no challenges in your life, you would be bored stiff or dead (which takes bored stiff to the maximum!).

A problem is nothing but concentrated opportunity!

NORMAN VINCENT PEALE

Anthony Robbins has a great metaphor to make this concept even clearer. If you wanted to build a bigger and stronger biceps muscle, how would you do it? By overloading the muscle—that is, by lifting progressively heavier weights in sets of ten to fifteen repetitions, three days a week for several weeks. That's how you sculpt a powerful biceps muscle.

You build your mental, emotional, and spiritual muscles the same way. Life puts changes in your path. These changes present challenges, which you overcome by making the correct choices that move you from where you are now to where you want to go. You use the challenges to grow as a person. Then, after you've grown in response to the challenges, what's life going to do one day later, one week later, or one month later? Let you rest on your laurels? Hardly.

Life will give you another challenge in the form of a change. What must you do to learn and grow continuously? Overcome challenges by making the correct change utilization choices!

The key to your universe is that you can choose!

CARL FREDERICK

CHALLENGE

by Nate Booth

A challenge is an invitation,

Not a warning or something bad.

It's an invitation to the dance of life,

A chance to learn and grow.

Are you going to accept and go?

Or decline and wish you had?

And watch as life offers it anew

To someone else instead?

Remember in Chapter 12 you learned about cycles? There's one more cycle I'd like to share with you now. I call it the Cycle of Life.

The Cycle of Life

The cycle of life has four stages: BE, DO, HAVE, and GIVE. Let's take a look at each stage, starting with BE.

BEing is where it all begins—when you are BEing resourceful, happy, or loving, for example, you will DO resourceful, happy, or loving things. Remember the last chapter, in which you learned the Nine Traits of Personal Change Mastery (BE grounded, BE a master of change utilization, BE flexible, etc.)? These traits are not just things you must DO; they go far deeper than that. They are the nine ways you will need to BE across the board in order to thrive in your rapidly changing world.

DO is the second stage of the Cycle of Life. Much of our lives is spent doing things; the question is, "Are we doing the things that are meaningful, that will make a difference for ourselves and others?" If your actions, your DOing, arise from empowering states of BEing, you will naturally choose to DO what is meaningful and important. I also believe that there is a higher power that will give you the power to run your Cycle of Life. It's vital that you tap into this power source on a regular basis.

HAVE is the third stage of the Cycle of Life. Most people focus almost exclusively on the HAVE stage, and forget they have to BE and DO first! When you consistently DO the right things, you will HAVE the things you desire in life. You will have all the relationships, emotions, and possessions that accompany a life well-lived.

Now that you HAVE what you desire, you can't stop there—you must move to the fourth stage of the cycle. You must GIVE from what you HAVE. And more important than giving anything material, you must GIVE to others your positive emotional states, like happiness, and love. You must GIVE away your support and knowledge. And yes, when appropriate, you may choose to GIVE your physical assets as well. Your goal in giving should always be to enable the recipients to BE more in their own lives.

Giving is a vital part of the Cycle of Life for two reasons. First, you will receive from life that which you give. When you give support, happiness, and love, for example, you will receive support, happiness, and love in your life because you will attract people and experiences that will enhance these positive emotions inside you. When you reflect a resourceful attitude to the world, you will attract the very resources you need—whether they be physical, emotional, or spiritual—that will move you toward your personal vision. When you give happiness, you will attract it; when you give love, you become a magnet for all the love in the world. And these gifts of life will enhance your BEing, and the Cycle of Life can begin anew with even greater power!

Second, when you GIVE to others in empowering ways, they will never BE the same. You will help enhance their BEing, and a new improved Cycle of Life will begin for them, allowing them to DO and HAVE more—and GIVE more to others as well. It looks like this:

The Interdependent Cycles of Life

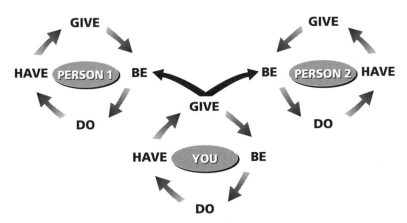

I hope that this book will be both a catalyst and a resource to enhance your Cycle of Life so you can BE, DO, and HAVE all the things you desire and deserve. I also hope that you will then GIVE to others in ways that enhance their Cycles of Life. When enough of us do this on a consistent basis, the synergy of these Cycles creates an expanding, upward spiral. And who knows how high we will go?

The Upward Spiral of Life

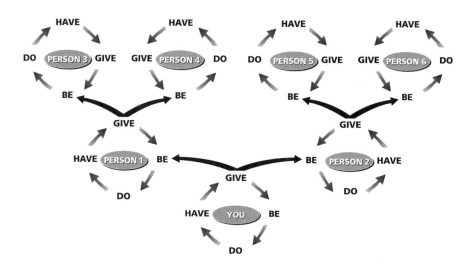

We must become the change we seek in the world.

MAHATMA GANDHI

To paraphrase the Roman statesman Seneca, God guides those who are willing and ready to change. Those who are not, God drags! Remember my friend Bob Weiland, the Vietnam vet who walked across the United States on his hands? Because he was willing and ready, Bob was guided to become a model of possibility for all of us. Bob had a purpose, a dream, a guide, and an unshakable spirit that inspired him to use change in his life to everyone's advantage.

Because he was willing and ready, Nelson Mandela was guided to become the symbol of freedom and leader for the people of South Africa. Because she was willing and ready, Mary Kay Ash was guided to create a company that has transformed the lives of millions of women and men, giving them a way to own their own successful businesses. Because he was willing and ready, Walt Disney was guided to create entertainment and happiness for people all around the world.

The thrill of living in today's world is that we can all be a Bob Weiland, a Nelson Mandela, a Mary Kay Ash, or a Walt Disney, each in our own way.

You can take your life from where you are right now, add the ingredients of constant change, and be guided toward your dreams with purpose and passion!

I trust this book will be one of your guides on that journey. I also trust you will let me know how your trip is progressing. Have a challenging, exhilarating, and rewarding journey of lifelong change!

WANT TO LEARN MORE?

To receive a complimentary copy of the Morning Questions card and other information to continue sharpening your change-mastery skills, call us at 800-445-8183, extension 6290.

To order additional copies of Thriving on Change *for your friends, family, and co-workers, the following quantity discounts are available.*

Quantity	Percent Discount
2–4	20%
5–49	30%
50–99	40%
100+	50%

Please call us at
800-445-8183, extension 6290!

ABOUT THE AUTHOR

For the past twenty-five years, Dr. Nate Booth has been relentlessly studying, applying, and coaching others in the art of thriving in times of rapid change. As the Head Corporate Trainer for the Anthony Robbins Companies of San Diego, Nate has worked closely with peak performance coach Anthony Robbins, creating and presenting a powerful series of training programs for organizations.

Nate received his D.D.S. degree from the University of Nebraska in 1971 and was in private dental practice for eight years. In 1983, he decided to switch careers and earned a master's degree in counseling. He began his association with Anthony Robbins in 1987. Nate has presented more than one thousand seminars, workshops, and training programs to audiences around the world. His clients include Aetna, Arthur Andersen, AT&T, Blue Cross–Blue Shield, Century 21, Eastman Kodak, Honeywell, IBM, *Inc.* Magazine, Kraft Foods, Mobil Oil, NASA, Norwest Bank, Prudential Insurance, Sanyo, Saturn Corporation, Siemens Corporation, University of California Irvine School of Medicine, University of South Carolina School of Business, Midwest Gas Association, U.S. West Direct, and the National Auto Dealers Association.

Nate is married and has three children—Chris, age 31, Emily, age 21, and Belinda, age 12. Nate, his wife Dawn, and Belinda live in Encinitas, California.

Corporate and Association Training Programs with Dr. Nate Booth

Invite Dr. Nate Booth to your corporation or association for a high energy, keynote presentation; an impactful half- or full-day workshop; or a comprehensive multi-day training program. Each topic can be customized for general audiences, salespeople, leaders, or managers. Dr. Booth is also available on a consulting basis to enhance your group's performance in the rapidly changing business world.

Thriving on Change:
The Art of Using Change to Your Advantage

Change Masters are a rare breed: They thrive on rapid change because they know it creates tremendous opportunities. Learn the skills to use any change to your advantage!

Everyone Is a Customer

In today's competitive business world, your external and internal customers are your most valuable asset. Discover how to give them the unique "customerized" service that will bring them back again and again!

Precision Service

What equals superb service is different for each individual. Discover your customers' unique service desires, and learn how to deliver the quality of service that will bring them back again and again!

Dream Quest

Walt Disney, John F. Kennedy, Mary Kay Ash, Nelson Mandela—they all had big dreams and made them come true. Now you can master the five steps all visionaries use to turn dreams into reality.

Elegant Influence

A different kind of "sales" program! Learn the psychological reasons people choose to take action so you can naturally enter the process and influence them to say yes. A must for anyone who wants to influence customers, teammates, employees, managers, children, etc.!

Busting Through Your Barriers: The Board-Breaking Experience

Use the metaphor of breaking wood karate-style to break through your self-imposed barriers. Create a life, group, or company that are masterpieces of action!

The Power of Synergy

Remember when you were part of a synergistic group that created outstanding results—and had a blast in the process? Learn the Nine Keys to Synergy to build more powerful, effective, and rewarding teams than ever before.

A group once stretched by a positive emotional experience, and given practical and powerful skills, never returns to its original dimensions!

DR. NATE BOOTH

To learn more, call 800-445-8183, extension 6290!

Here's what people are saying about Dr. Nate Booth's corporate and association training programs:

"Congratulations, you were rated the number one speaker (out of fifty speakers) at *Inc.* Magazine's Fifth Annual Conference on Customer Service. Tremendous job!"

KEVIN GILLIGAN, CONFERENCE PRODUCER
Inc. *Magazine, Boston, MA*

"I have seen motivational presentations on topics before, but in my opinion, your enthusiasm and technique are second to none!"

ANN KROUPA, VICE PRESIDENT, SPECIALIZED MARKETS
AT&T, Basking Ridge, NJ

"The evaluations are in. You were the hit of the conference! That's truly outstanding when you consider this group of CEOs and upper-level managers see a lot of professional presenters each year."

RICK HINKIE, PRESIDENT
Midwest Gas Association, Minneapolis, MN

"In my twenty-five years as a conference organizer, I have never seen a speaker achieve perfect marks from an audience—until you came along!"

JIM COULSON, DIRECTOR OF EDUCATION
University of California Irvine Medical Center, Irvine, CA

"Outstanding! Your presentation to NTS senior management was timely, enthusiastic, and right on."

DIANA INGRAHAM, CONFERENCE CHAIR
Norwest Technical Services, Minneapolis, MN

"YES!! What a dynamic speaker you are! I have never had the privilege of listening to a more motivating talk in the history of my career."

CARMELA PORTER, EXECUTIVE DIRECTOR
Professional Association of Health Care Office Managers, Pensacola, FL

"Little did I believe you could keep our high energy group contained and excited for a full four hours. Yet your material, coupled with your delivery style of speed, wit, and participation, kept all two hundred riveted and involved."

DICK MORGAN, DIRECTOR OF MARKETING
Milgard Windows, Tacoma, WA

"Congratulations on being rated the number one speaker (out of twenty) at our recent convention. I heard nothing but wonderful comments about your program!"

KATHI BROWN, WORKSHOP COORDINATOR
National Automobile Dealers Association, Washington, DC

"If you want a speaker who will both inspire your audience and give them specific tools to improve their performance, Nate Booth is the man you are looking for. Don't miss out on the chance to hear one of our nation's finest speakers!"

ANTHONY ROBBINS, PEAK PERFORMANCE COACH
Author, Unlimited Power *and* Awaken the Giant Within

Anthony Robbins' Programs

"There are no better experiential programs available anywhere.
Give yourself the gift of seeing Anthony Robbins live!"

DR. NATE BOOTH

THE COMPETITIVE EDGE—
The Power of Personal and Professional Influence

In a single intensive day with the world's foremost peak performance
coach, Anthony Robbins, you'll model the techniques of the world's
most successful salespeople—those earning a minimum of a quarter
of a million dollars per year in personal income. Gain years of
concentrated experience and expertise in just a few hours!

UNLEASH THE POWER WITHIN—
The Ultimate Experience of Transformation and Lasting Change

In one life-changing weekend, you'll not only master key communication
skills, beliefs, and physiology—you'll literally condition your mind and
body to consistently react with power and focus in any situation.
Learn how to break through to ultimate success!

MASTERY UNIVERSITY®

The ultimate experience: seventeen days with Anthony Robbins and the finest masters from around the world—showing you personally how to transform your emotions, your physical health, your relationships, your finances, your time, and your life—forever! The three sessions include:

DATE WITH DESTINY™

Discover exactly why you do what you do—and create a life plan where every thought, feeling, belief, and action pulls you toward the destiny you truly desire!

LIFE MASTERY

In nine days with Anthony Robbins and the finest masters and coaches in the world, you will learn how to achieve massive success in every major area of your life. There is no finer training available anywhere!

WEALTH MASTERY™

The psychology of money . . . the six financial dreams . . . evaluating the best investments for long-term value and immediate cash flow . . . creating an achievable plan to become financially independent for life . . . Spend four days with Anthony Robbins and other masters learning the secrets of true wealth.

(NOTE: *Each session of Mastery University can be taken as an independent program. Significant package price incentives available. Call for a detailed prospectus.*)

To learn more, call 800-898-8669!

SOURCES

"America, Land of the Shaken," *Business Week*, 11 March 1996, 64–65.

Anderson, Duncan Maxwell and Michael Warshaw, "*Success* Magazine's 7th Annual Renegades," *Success Magazine*, January/February 1994, 39–44.

Barker, Joel Arthur. *Future Edge: Discovering the New Paradigms of Success*. New York: William Morrow and Company, 1992.

Belton, Beth, "Degree-Based Earnings Gap Grows Quickly," *USA Today*, 9 February 1996.

Biro, Brian D. *Beyond Success—The 15 Secrets of a Winning Life*. Hamilton, MT: Pygmalion Press, 1995.

Blanchard, Ken and Sheldon Bowles. *Raving Fans—A Revolutionary Approach to Customer Service*. New York: William Morrow and Company, 1993.

Bridges, William. *JobShift: How to Prosper in a Workplace Without Jobs*. Reading, MA: Addison-Wesley Publishing Company, 1994.

———. *Managing Transitions: Making the Most of Change*. Reading, MA: Addison-Wesley Publishing Company, 1991.

———. *Transitions—Making Sense of Life's Changes*. Reading, MA: Addison-Wesley Publishing Company, 1980.

Burrus, Daniel with Roger Gittines. *Technotrends: How to Use Technology to Go Beyond Your Competition*. New York: HarperBusiness, 1993.

Celente, Gerald with Tom Milton, *Trend Tracking*. New York: Warner Books, 1991.

Collins, James C., "Change Is Good—But First, Know What Should Never Change," *Fortune*, 29 May 1995, 141.

——— and Jerry I. Porras. *Built to Last: Successful Habits of Visionary Companies*. New York: HarperBusiness, 1994.

Conner, Daryl R. *Managing at the Speed of Change*. New York: Villard Books, 1993.

Covey, Stephen R. *Principle-Centered Leadership*. Provo, UT: The Institute for Principle Centered Leadership, 1990.

———. *The 7 Habits of Highly Effective People*. New York: Simon and Schuster, 1989.

Dent, Harry S. Jr. *The Great Boom Ahead*. New York: Hyperion, 1993.

Farkas, Charles M. and Philippe de Bacher. *Maximum Leadership*. New York: Henry Holt and Company, 1996.

Farrell, Christopher, Michael J. Mandel and Joseph Weber, "Riding High: Corporate America Now Has an Edge Over its Global Rivals," *Business Week*, 9 October 1995, 134–146.

Fleschner, Malcom, "Paranoia Principle," *Personal Selling Power*, October 1995, 12–18.

Hammer, Michael and James Champy. *Reengineering the Corporation: A Manifesto for Business Revolution*. New York: HarperBusiness, 1993.

Handy, Charles. *The Age of Paradox*. Boston: Harvard Business School Press, 1994.

Hof, Robert D. and Amy Cortese, "Browsing for a Bruising?" *Business Week*, 11 March 1996, 82–84.

Kotkin, Joel, "The Innovation Upstarts," *Inc.*, January 1989, 70–74.

Kriegel, Robert J. and Louis Patler. *If It Ain't Broke...BREAK IT!* New York: Warner Books, 1991.

McHugh, Josh, "Holy Cow, No One's Done This!" *Forbes*, 3 June 1996, 122–128.

Morgan, Peter Scott. *The Unwriten Rules of the Game*. New York: McGraw-Hill, 1994.

Morrison, Ian. *The Second Curve*. New York: Ballantine Books, 1996.

Naisbitt, John. *Megatrends*. New York: Warner Books, 1988.

Pennar, Karen, Susan B. Garland, and Elizabeth Roberts, "Economic Anxiety," *Business Week*, 11 March 1996, 50–56.

Peters, Tom. *Embracing Chaos*. Chicago: Nightingale-Conant, 1993. Audiotapes.

———. *The Pursuit of WOW!* New York: Vintage Books, 1994.

————. *The Tom Peters Seminar—Crazy Times Call for Crazy Organizations*. New York: Vintage Books, 1994.

Popcorn, Faith. *The Popcorn Report*. New York: Doubleday, 1991.

————. *Clicking*. New York: Harper Collins, 1996.

Pritchett, Price. *New Work Habits for a Radically Changing World*. Dallas: Pritchett & Associates, Inc., 1994.

Price Waterhouse Change Integration Team. *Better Change*. Burr Ridge, IL: Irwin Professional Publishing, 1995.

Robbins, Anthony. *Awaken the Giant Within*. New York: Summit Books, 1991.

————. *Unlimited Power*. New York: Fawcett Columbine, 1986.

Schiller, Zachary, "The Revolving Door at Rubbermaid," *Business Week*, 18 September 1995, 80–84.

Sheehy, Gail. *New Passages*. New York: Random House, 1995.

Sprout, Alison L., "Packard Bell Sells More PCs in the U.S. than Anyone. So Just Who are These Guys?" *Fortune*, 12 June 1995, 82–88.

Tracy, Brian. *Action Strategies for Personal Achievement*. Chicago: Nightingale-Conant, 1993. Audiotapes.

Treacy, Michael and Fred Wiersema. *The Discipline of Market Leaders*. Reading, MA: Addison-Wesley Publishing Company, 1995.

Thomas, Bob. *Walt Disney—An American Original*. New York: Hyperion, 1994.

Wieland, Bob. *One Step at a Time: The Incredible True Story of Bob Wieland*. Grand Rapids, MI: Zondervan Publishing Company, 1989.

Willette, Anne, "Baby Boomers Resist Retiring as Golden Oldies," *USA Today*, 29 April 1996.

Williams, W. W., "Game for Growth: Nintendo Co. Ltd.," *Hemispheres*, April 1996, 29–32.

INDEX